BIBLICAL
FAITH
MEETS FINANCIAL
STRATEGY

HOW TO LAY A SOLID
FOUNDATION FOR PROSPERITY

Biblical Faith Meets Financial Strategy

How to Lay a Solid Foundation for Prosperity

SECOND EDITION

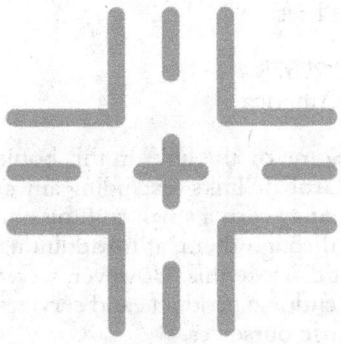

INTERSECTION

Where God's Wealth Meets God's Wisdom

JOHNNY MCWILLIAMS

Zero In Financial Press

Myrtle Beach, South Carolina

Zero In Financial Press
PO BOX 1718
Myrtle Beach, SC 29578
United States of America

Full Disclosure: Some of the links in this book and related
materials may be affiliate links (excluding any and all links to
Amazon), and we may earn a small commission when you
make a purchase through them, at no additional cost to you. By
FTC law we must disclose this. However, we want to assure
you that we only endorse products and services we believe in
and would or do use ourselves.

Biblical Faith Meets Financial Strategy, How to Lay a Solid
Foundation for Prosperity / Series: INTERSECTION, Where
God's Wealth Meets God's Wisdom / Johnny McWilliams,
author — 2nd ed.

Hardback ISBN-13: 978-1-954485-07-5
Paperback ISBN-13: 978-1-954485-05-1
E-book (EPUB) ISBN-13: 978-1-954485-06-8
E-book (PDF) ISBN-13: 978-1-954485-08-2
Library of Congress Control Number: 2022907457

Access free resources mentioned in this book:
intersection.zeroinfinancial.com

Editor: Fleur Marie Vaz, fleurmarievaz@gmail.com
Additional Editing: Melanie Brown
Cover image design: Edgar Rios, edgrrr5@gmail.com

Contents

Dedication

I dedicate this book series to my Lord and Savior, Jesus Christ, who has carried me, walked with me, and led me all the way to completion. Thank You for always being the God who always keeps His promises.

> *And the Lord, he it is that doth go before thee; he will be with thee, he will not fail thee, neither forsake thee: fear not, neither be dismayed (Deuteronomy 31:8).*

Acknowledgments

I want to acknowledge and thank my best friend and incredible wife, Christine. Your undying support never ceases to amaze me. You have stood by me through it all. I couldn't have finished this project without you.

Thank you to my children, Seth and Paige. I love you and am so proud to be your dad. Your faith in Christ and success in life have been a beautiful display of God's grace.

Thank you to my parents, Clovers and Val McWilliams. You have always been a rock of consistent encouragement, believing in me throughout the decades. You both have faithfully studied the Word of God and have inspired me to do the same. Your prayers have kept blessings pouring out upon my life.

Thank you to my Pastor for over a decade, Al Toledo, for your powerful teaching and ministry that will always have a lasting influence on my business and writing. And to my current Pastor, Chris Honeycutt, who has been abundantly supportive as I worked through the last twelve months of this project.

Free Resources

To help you Zero In on the INTERSECTION where God's Wealth meets God's Wisdom, download the free resources from the INTERSECTION Resource Page:

intersection.zeroinfinancial.com

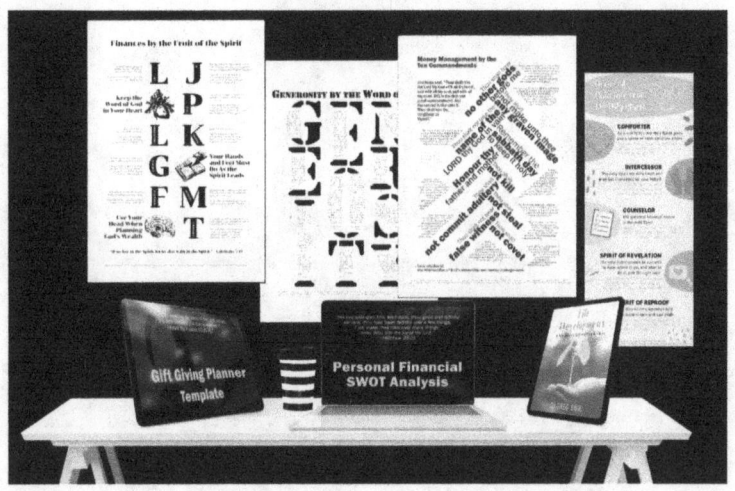

- **BOOK:** Life Development—A New Believer's Guide to Growing in Christ

- **INFOGRAPHIC:** Financial Guidance from the Holy Spirit

- **POSTER:** Finances by the Fruit of the Spirit

- **WORKBOOK:** Personal Financial SWOT Analysis

- **POSTER:** Money Management by the Ten Commandments

- **WORKBOOK:** Gift Giving Planner Template

- **POSTER:** Generosity by the Word of God

INTRODUCTION

Taking Aim

Imagine yourself at the shooting range, aiming at a target. To ensure your aim is accurate, you look for a calibrated point of reference. Scopes use two engraved lines to give the operator a single place to focus on when aiming at a target. The two lines cross at this spot and create an intersecting pattern known as crosshairs.

So, when setting your sights with your weapon, you typically would use crosshairs. There is a reference for the horizontal plane and for the vertical plane. The purpose is to align the crosshairs, where the two lines intersect, with the bullseye. Aiming to hit the bullseye requires precision and, using the simple principle of intersecting lines, you can easily pinpoint that target.

In our case, those two planes are God's Wealth and God's Wisdom. Once you have these two crosshairs in focus and zeroed in, you can aim right at the center of your target and hit it consistently.

When peering through your financial scope towards the future, there are several marks you need to target. For this book series, *INTERSECTION—Where God's Wealth Meets God's Wisdom,* I will focus on a few of these targets.

However, before you focus on the bullseye, you must ensure the crosshairs are zeroed-in or correctly calibrated to guarantee hitting your target.

This book series is for anyone who wants to understand the foundational principles of money. Each book is genuinely a one-size-fits-all because it reveals foundational principles instead of custom strategies. It doesn't matter your current age, wage, or stage. These are vital truths for every individual's financial life. When you have a skewed understanding of the fundamentals, you never master the art. And in this book, I will explain how a foolproof financial strategy always begins and ends with biblical faith.

As a financial coach, I sit down and help people face to face, and when they need a hug, shoulder to shoulder. It may be online or in-person, but in either case, my job is to listen, teach, and help guide them through a personal, tailor-made plan.

While the principles apply to all, this plan is *their* plan, unique to their situation, goals, and aspirations. Zero In Financial® has a mission to help every client, reader, customer, follower, and fan zero in.

We will walk with you as you
RECOVER from past money mistakes,
GROW your present pocketbook position, and
ZERO IN on your future financial fortune,
ultimately leaving a lasting legacy of love.

You need to RECOVER, GROW, and ZERO IN, but in your unique personal way. Although your resulting strategy is custom tailored, each must stay rooted in the same foundational principles found in the Word of God.

This book series will take you step by step through the foundational truths I use every day in coaching. Customization builds on top of these basic principles. Coaching is less about me talking and more about me actively listening. Everyone needs a mentor and coach, and I fill those voids as I encourage and guide. Even with the plethora of financial challenges you likely face, it comes down to the basics. When it's time to teach, this series is the playbook.

The Chicago Tribune published an article titled *A Coach In Your Corner* where someone asked, "Who, exactly, seeks out a coach?" The response: "Winners who want even more out of life."[1]

Take sports, for example. I notice the best athletes go further. It may seem that the best don't have to prove anything and therefore don't have to prepare for the game. But just the opposite is true. The best athletes practice more, train more, and seek more coaching than the average player.

Here is the secret to being the best version of you: spend the most time practicing the rudiments. Yes, the basics. The greatest coaches have their star players running wind sprints, shooting free-throws, and perfecting the bunt. The key to being the best you can be is getting good at the basics. As Larry Bird, three-time National Basketball Association champion, said, "First master the fundamentals."

Finances are no different, and there are many parallels between physical fitness and fiscal fitness. Let me be your mentor, your guide, your coach in this walk towards financial freedom. Take your time and digest the foundational truths in this book series. If you do, I promise you will be ready for game time and ready to take your best shot at each target.

If this series is the foundation of your financial plan, then this book is the cornerstone. You must begin here. It will impact your financial plan and set the stage for the books that follow because it covers the most important aspects of managing wealth. If you don't pick up these keystone truths, it will be tough to apply the principles in later volumes.

Again, if you want to pinpoint your financial destiny, you need to zero-in on your target, not someone else's mark. As I mentioned, the simple tool needed for pinpoint accuracy is the crosshairs. One of the most critical steps is knowing where you are aiming. I will walk you through discovering your target so you can zero in with confidence.

The blessings come where the two lines meet. So, it's time you have a focal point; let's reveal the perfect intersection of God's Wealth and God's Wisdom for your life. If you are ready to construct a financial strategy according to the Word of God and live a prosperous life, read on!

Part I

Radical Relationships

Live in Christ Jesus

Don't worry; you didn't pick up the wrong book. This book is about wealth, prosperity, and living the dream. And the first chapter will reveal the most important step. If you don't address this first, nothing else really matters. I'm referring to debt. But I am not speaking of financial debt.

I'm speaking of addressing the very center point of your crosshairs. It's the target you are aiming at. Who or what is at your center?

In *God's Ownership Meets Money Management*, I look back to humankind at the beginning of time because a study of the past is an indispensable exercise in understanding the present. But, I want to point out here how people have been struggling with greed, doubt, fear, and selfishness from day one. Our very nature is to gravitate towards bad feelings, toxic thoughts, and evil desires.

But, before I get ahead of myself, let's talk about dreams.

Living the Dream

What does the phrase "Living the Dream" really mean? I have used this response when someone asks how I am doing. But because it is so overused, I don't think they believed me. In fact, when someone responds to me with this line, I always wonder if they are truly living what they dream about and if their dream is intensely worth living.

My goal is to begin this book by offering you a polarizing thought that separates the mundane from the profound. The most perfect and prosperous life is the one in which Jesus Christ is at the center. This means that, if Jesus is not at the intersection of your dreams (all that you want, hope for, and aspire to have out of life), and the way you live life (your daily actions, habits, and motives), your life will not be a dream come true.

Some tell me they don't have a dream, declaring that they don't have big goals and objectives in life. Being complacent and letting someone else provide for them is perfectly fine, they say. But I don't believe them.

Everyone has a dream. For some, it may bubble out in every word and action. Others may only reveal their vision when asked about it, and even then, forming the words may not be easy. In contrast, there are those who won't even communicate such things, or even worse, don't even recognize their deepest desires. One reason is because they have become numb from the scars of the past. We all have scars from the past. Depending on how deep, scar tissue could be the thing covering up some, most, or all of our passion.

Scars or not, you still have a dream. Everyone has had a different path, and we are all made for various purposes. Your Heavenly Father who made you embedded that dream within you. So, if you want a dream worth living, focus your thoughts on the One who gave you life.

I can always tell if someone has their crosshairs correctly aligned with their deepest heart's desires. The tell-tale sign is always their view of the world, of humanity, and of God. When someone has their faith rooted in the Bible, they have big dreams; they have a smile on their face even in times of difficulty, and they never give up despite their circumstances.

When someone has lost that faith or has never been a believer, their demeanor is different. They seem to always be in the middle of an issue; they seem defeated, and their hopes and dreams are like spoiled milk. The rollercoaster of living, events and situations in the news, and every obstacle and challenge seem to beat them up and keep them down. They keep saying, "I just can't get ahead."

Then there are those who fall in the middle. They may not be dealing with severe issues like depression or hopelessness; nevertheless they struggle. Someone may have hurt them in the past, or they went through an extremely difficult patch of life. It may have been the loss of a job, divorce, bankruptcy, the pandemic, just to name a few. (I know because I've been through all of the above.)

So they are hanging on, but only day by day. If a major issue were to crop up, everything they have worked so hard to build would tumble to the ground. Every time life happens, they get knocked off their financial course.

If you would like help in targeting your life's dream, I will share with you the perfect way to aim. And when you implement this strategy, even the winds of life will not affect your focus on the target.

God desires that you have the prescribed portion you need in order to fulfill His purpose for your life: the dream. So, first, you need to fix your perspective on the One who provides all. Then, and only then, will you find peace, joy, happiness,… genuinely living the dream.

Check out this scripture written by the Apostle Peter. The International Children's Bible puts this passage in a way that addresses the heart of the matter:

"To you who have received a faith as valuable as ours. You received that faith because our God and Savior Jesus Christ is fair and does what is right. Grace and peace be given to you more and more. **You will have grace and peace because you truly know God and Jesus our Lord. Jesus has the power of God.** His power has given us everything we need to live and to serve God. We have these things because we know him. Jesus called us by his glory and goodness. **Through his glory and goodness, he gave us the very great and rich gifts he promised us**. With those gifts you can share in God's nature" (2 Peter 1:1-4a ICB).

So, what does a Christ-centered life have to do with living the dream? Everything! Just wait; you will see.

Let Christ Be Lord and Savior

It happens to all of us. I know you see no evil in the eyes of a sweet newborn baby. But how long does it take for that child to get into trouble? Not long. As soon as it can crawl, it's exploring its little world and heads for the staircase!

The parents love their child so much that they put up restrictions and boundaries for its safety. And the child instinctively and almost immediately tries to breach those safeguards. So what do the parents do? Protect, rescue, and teach.

As your guide on this journey to financial freedom, I, too, want to make this assertion: there is nothing more important than for you to understand your desperate need for The Savior.

The most significant intersection in history was the cross.

Just pick up a newspaper (do they have those anymore?), or turn on your preferred news video stream, and you will see what happens when men and women abandon their Savior for the lusts of their flesh. The further entire households, communities, countries and the world move from Godly boundaries and safeguards, the more dreadful things become.

Though society often calls it by nice names like "wrong choices," this reality is sin. When Jesus gave us the model we call the Lord's Prayer, He describes sin as debt: "…And **forgive us our debts**, as we forgive our debtors. And lead us not into temptation, but deliver us from evil: For thine is the kingdom, and the power, and the glory, forever. Amen" (Matthew 6:9-13).

John W. Ritenbaugh says in his message, *Passover, Obligation, and Love*, "It is interesting to note in the model prayer of Matthew 6:9-13 that sin is expressed through the image of debt, a true metaphor. Duty neglected, a debt to God, must be discharged by a penalty. All have sinned and the wages or penalty is death (Romans 3:23; 6:23). We are all under a peculiar form of indebtedness which we cannot pay and still have hope!"[1]

Do you realize the seriousness of sin in your life? It is a debt you cannot pay off, and the penalty for not paying it off is death. Yes, it is that serious, and it may seem hopeless until you understand God made a way for us all to be sin debt free. God established a strategy for you and me to live the dream not only here on earth but for life-everlasting.

Are you ready to be debt-free, that is, cleansed from sin? Salvation is free, for the price has already been paid by Jesus: all you must do is declare Jesus as your Lord and Savior and repent of your sins. You will be made new; you will be spiritually born again.

In Ted E. Bowling's sermon, *Sticks and Stones*, he states:

> *Our sins are debts to God, which we, the debtors,*
> *cannot pay. God is willing to wipe our slates clean*
> *if we humble ourselves before Him. We ask for*
> *forgiveness for our sins, and by so doing, we*
> *acknowledge that there is no other way to get rid of*
> *sin but through the sacrifice of Jesus Christ.*[2]

You must therefore zero-in or center your life on Christ, not self. The most selfish act anyone could do is to think they are the center of their world. An essential first step to living the dream is putting your life and need for a Savior in proper perspective.

In the sermon *Let Christ Be the Centre of Your Life*, Pastor Zac Poonen preached:

> *Repentance means turning from our old way of*
> *life. It means a whole lot more than just giving up*
> *some bad habits, like drinking, gambling, and the*
> *like. Our old way of life is a self-centered life; and*
> *repentance means saying, "Lord, I'm tired of*

being centered in myself and I want to turn to You
now and to be centered in You." ³

Don't worry if you think you are not ready to
surrender. No one ever is. You don't deserve forgiveness,
either. There is nothing you can do or give to earn it. All
you need to know is that there is only one way, and you can
have it today.

"We believe that we are all saved the same way, **by the**
undeserved grace of the Lord Jesus" (Acts of the
Apostles 15:11 NLT).

I want nothing more than to know that this book has
helped you see your need to be born again, made whole,
and freed from the debt of sin. You were born once
through natural means; now you will be born a second
time into a new life in Christ Jesus through the Spirit of
God.

If you are not born again and want to make heaven
your home, I would like to lead you in prayer.

There is nothing mysterious about these words, and
you must mean them wholeheartedly; so, please, make
them your own. I only want to provide you a template, a
place to start, if you don't know what to say. These words
are from the sinner's prayer that Billy Graham would use
to lead someone as they pray for salvation.

So, bow your head and your heart, and if you believe
these words, Jesus will forever change your life.

*Dear Lord Jesus, I know that I am a sinner, and
I ask for Your forgiveness. I believe You died for
my sins and rose from the dead. I turn from my
sins and invite You to come into my heart and
life. I want to trust and follow You as my Lord
and Savior. In Your Name. Amen*[4]

If you have made this decision today, please let me
know, plus I would like to send you a gift to help you with
your walk with Christ.

**The gift I would like to send you is an
indispensable resource. My dear friend,
accountability partner, and fellow
author, Pastor D. Greg Ebie has
allowed me to distribute his book,
"Life Development—A New Believer's
Guide to Growing in Christ," to anyone
who declares their life in Christ. I
would like to thank him for writing this
amazing book but also for allowing me
to provide it to you.**

**I really wanted to share something
that would help you grow your faith in
Jesus Christ because Biblical Faith is
the only way to develop a reliable
Financial Strategy. Get ready to be
challenged as you work your way**

through Pastor Greg's foundational guide.

Grab your copy of this study guide and have your Bible in hand! Download it today: salvation.zeroinfinancial.com[5]

Let Christ Be Servant and King

How did Jesus become our Savior when He is the King of kings? What kind of leader sacrifices his life for his people? And why was there no other way?

God is perfect in every way. He cannot sin. So, when we entered into sin, beginning with Adam, God had already provided the means to rescue His creation out of the devil's clutches. Our loving Creator had made a way for us to come back to Him. He does not want a single person to perish. But He is a just God and must judge sin as sin. And, as we see in scripture, the penalty for sin is death.

What is death? I am not referring to death as in your body reaching its expiration date and being buried in the ground. No, what I mean by death is eternal separation from God. Being forever separated from our Maker would be the worst perpetual existence ever. You don't want that.

How does God want the debt of sin to be paid? Through the principle He has established from the beginning: blood sacrifice. In the Old Testament, a spotless innocent animal had to die and shed its blood to

When Christ

intersects with our

circumstance,

our situation receives

a course correction.

cover someone's sin. But this was always a temporary solution. There needed to be a permanent sacrifice.

So God the Father sent His Only Son to die once and for all. Jesus the King humbled Himself by coming to earth and dying a sinner's death, even though He is perfect in every way. He is sinless because He is God; and yet, because He is also man, He represents humanity in all our frailty before the Father.

The most significant intersection in history was at the cross. Jesus laid down His life for you and me as a servant. Then, He rose to power to His rightful place as King of kings. Finally, He sent the Holy Spirit to comfort, guide, and empower us in every circumstance and challenge we face. True freedom begins where Servant intersects with King.

When you become free, you are free indeed. The Bible says that Jesus came "to minister, and to give his life a ransom for many" (Mark 10:45b).

So, as Christ ministers to you, not only will you get to learn great wisdom, and this book will explore much of His wisdom concerning finances, but you will be set free from captivity. Jesus paid the ransom.

When you watch a movie in which a ransom is paid, it is typically "money that is paid to someone so that they will release a person who is being kept as a prisoner by them."[6] But there is no sum of money that could pay off the debt of your sin. Only the blood of the innocent Lamb would suffice.

The chains of sin were holding you captive. Now that you have prayed that prayer, accepting His sacrifice as Servant and positioning Jesus as King, you can begin living the dream.

Now, I hope you see this as the single most important thing you ever do in your life. I pray you realize how worthless money and possessions are when compared to the gift of God's new life. You will be blessed beyond belief by the rest of this book if you apply this first principle wholly to your life.

Let Christ Be Master and Teacher

Now I understand how hesitant you might feel about having The Perfect One enter your circumstances. You are not quite ready for any radical changes; you are caught up in other things and don't have the space right now. But let's face it. Living without Jesus is tiring. Without Him, we could end up going around in circles or in an undesirable direction.

But, once we eagerly surrender to the One who created us in His image to live under His protection, we will tap into that life of abundance even now, for He said that He came to give us life and even more abundantly (see John 10:10).

I meet so many people who want to learn financial strategy apart from Biblical faith. And, because I know that this will not lead to genuine fortune, I refuse to teach them to think this way. I am not saying that strategy without faith will be all bad. Many people find luxury and comfort on the road without faith. But that falls short of the blessing that God has prepared for you, which begins with receiving His new life. Again, the right path is not one that guarantees no trials or hurdles, for God is also at work on your character.

Try to envision your financial life as a boat; your aim is to get it on the right course. There may be calmer waters in another direction, but it will lead you to a place you didn't want to go. Your financial boat will only end up at your dream destination once you allow Jesus into your vessel.

Check out this Bible passage: "So when they had rowed about five and twenty or thirty furlongs, they see Jesus walking on the sea, and drawing nigh unto the ship: and they were afraid. But he saith unto them, It is I; be not afraid. **Then they willingly received him into the ship: and immediately the ship was at the land whither they went**" (John 6:19-21).

Let's put ourselves in the boat situation where the waves of financial adversity threaten to overwhelm us. So what options do we have?

Option 1—Work hard *without Jesus* in your boat, and you will get nowhere fast. Struggle with every financial challenge, stress about how you will reach your destination, and strain as you row against the waves. Or, at best, end up at the wrong destination.

Option 2—Let Jesus into your boat. Arrive at your destination.

Struggle, stress, and strain? Or salvation and sincere satisfaction? Your choice.

When we allow Christ to be the Captain of our ship, we are declaring Him as Master of everything that controls us. The ways of the Master are beyond our comprehension.

"For my thoughts are not your thoughts, neither are your ways my ways, saith the Lord. For as the heavens are higher than the earth, **so are my ways higher than your ways,** and my thoughts than your thoughts" (Isaiah 55:8-9).

We read here that there is nothing like the thoughts of the Master. His wisdom surpasses understanding, so it would be best to call Him Teacher.

My brother, my sister, let me assure you of this. If you have said that prayer, asking Jesus to be your Savior, you are now not only a child of the Living God, but you also have access to the One who knows all things and can do all things. All this financial stuff will be a piece of cake if we allow Him to be Master and Teacher of all.

When Christ intersects with our circumstance, our situation receives a course correction. A boat heading off-course is in danger of not reaching its intended destination, or worse, running aground. Every vessel has a navigation system or pilot whose job is to course-correct.

Jesus is the most reliable, accurate navigation system ever, and there is no competition.

Be sure to get your free copy of
Life Development—A New Believer's Guide to Growing In Christ
salvation.zeroinfinancial.com[5]

CHAPTER TWO

Not So Religious

Now that I know you are a child of God, I can write to you as my fellow sister or brother in Christ. That's a big deal. Jesus is all about relationships, not religion. If you did not pray that prayer, don't fret; this chapter will be just as beneficial.

Most of us have grown up hearing a whole lot of religious chatter and very little about the privilege we have of being in relationship with God Almighty. All our notions of God consist of a bunch of rules and regulations that we don't want to follow because there is no conviction behind them. With no proper understanding of

27

who He is, church, the Bible, prayer, and all that other "God stuff" is nothing but an inconvenience in our self-centered plans.

But what if I told you that you may not have the correct prospective? Read this chapter with an open mind and an open heart. By the end, I pray you not only realize financial freedom but a freedom to enter into the presence of the God of everything.

Relationship Over Religion

As you saw in the previous chapter, Jesus died for you so you could have a right relationship with God in His fullness (Father, Son, and Holy Spirit). He wants to be near you. God wants to be involved in every aspect of your life. God is a personal God. He is not distant. You can have an intimate relationship with your Maker, Savior, and Comforter. Living in this New Testament time means we have direct access to the Almighty!

In the Old Testament, that is B.C.—Before Christ—there is a book, which is all about a man called Job. The book of Job is one of my favorite books because it is a mysterious yet powerful, revealing, and humbling study of God in relation to man.

Job was a God-fearing and prosperous man, who was blessed with seven children and great material possessions. But one day, everything went, including his health. While his friends accused him of sin and his wife taunted him to curse God and die, Job maintained his innocence. He did not curse God either but sought Him to know why.

Some of Job's last words before God responded to him are so profound in their yearning to know the truth. In a state of so much misery and despair, Job says: "I need someone to mediate between God and me, as a person mediates between friends" (Job 16:21 NLT).

Isn't that all our heart's desire, our life's greatest need? Someone to present our case to a higher authority?

But his desire and request were not fulfilled immediately. His friends failed him and no one spoke up for him or comforted him. But in the end, God Himself visited him and exonerated him. Just as God defended Job, we don't have to yearn for such a mediator in our lostness.

Jesus is that person who mediates on our behalf. He has bridged that gap between the perfect Father and our flawed humanity. He is the Great Mediator. Now we can boldly make our petitions known before the throne of grace. Now we know that all good things come to us from the Giver of Life and be grateful for that.

Having a healthy perspective of possessions means thanking God for all He has given you, from morning to evening. Wake up praising and worshiping the Lord. Go to bed thanking Him for all He has allowed you to have, do, and be.

The Bible tells us that when Jesus ascended to heaven after He rose from the dead, He seated Himself at the right hand of God. In that place of power, He will take your petitions and stand in your place, ever ready to plead your case to the Father and defend you.

Only Jesus can fulfill this role because He is spotless and yet one of us: "There is one God and one Mediator who can reconcile God and humanity—the man Christ Jesus" (1 Timothy 2:5 NLT).

The Bible says He is continually in that role interceding for us to God: "He lives forever to intercede with God on their behalf" (Hebrews 7:25 NLT).

Being close to God ultimately means sensing God's presence all day and in every part of your day. I recommend you get a copy of *The Practice of the Presence of God* by Brother Lawrence[1]. He talks about being as close to God while working as he is on his knees.

If you were brought up in church like I was, recognizing all the policies, rules, and regulations, you might have missed the most crucial aspect of Christianity: having a right relationship with Jesus Christ. It will completely change your perspective. (I'll speak more about the church later in this chapter.)

Here is the difference: religion is all about what you can and cannot do, while relationship is all about who you are, and more importantly, whose you are. If your parents' house worked like religion, you would have had to earn your way back into the family whenever you did something naughty. Instead, a healthy upbringing would have included repercussions for disobeying, for example, loss of some of your freedoms, but you would never doubt your relationship with mom and dad.

Fritz Chery writes in the blog post, *Religion vs Relationship with God:*

> *Christianity says that you can't do. You have to trust in the One who has done it for you… Every other religion in the world teaches a works-based salvation. Christianity is the only religion in the world where you are justified by grace through faith in Christ alone. Religion keeps you in chains, but Christ has set us free.*[2]

God is a loving Father, and because He loves, He also corrects. There are real repercussions when we go astray. But when you are secure in His love for you, you can humble yourself, ask for forgiveness, and feel the relationship's freedom.

You didn't have to jump through hoops for your parents to feed you, clothe you, or buy you stuff you want. You may not have gotten everything you wanted, but any healthy household furnishes everything you need. This natural response to provide comes from God, but He does it ever better.

He is a generous and loving Father, and He is wealthy! "But my **God shall supply all your need according to his riches** in glory by Christ Jesus" (Philippians 4:19).

So, does that mean once you get saved, you can do whatever you want? Well, just because you are a part of your mother's house, do you treat her home however you like? No, we would call that being a spoiled brat.

Why not lie to mom and steal from dad? Because you love them back. You have a free will, but you obey authority because of respect. You obey your parents because you love them, not because of a demand.

Because of your relationship with God and your love for Him, you obey Him. And just like growing up in your parents' house, if you don't obey, you only hurt yourself.

I meet many people who do everything but obey the Word of God and then wonder why they don't prosper. As Zechariah said to the people, "Why do you disobey the Lord's commands and keep yourselves from prospering?" (2 Chronicles 24:20b NLT)

God has given us loving guidance to obey; this includes financial strategy. The foundation of all His instruction is found in the #1 Best-Selling Book of all time: The Bible.

Why the Bible

God has laid out what some call the Basic Instructions Before Leaving Earth (B.I.B.L.E.). When you need help, pray indeed, but don't forget to go to the reference manual.

> *All scripture is given by inspiration of God, and*
> *is profitable for doctrine, for reproof, for correction,*
> *for instruction in righteousness (2 Timothy 3:16).*

I believe a healthy spiritual diet includes reading your Bible every day. It will bless every aspect of your life—and that certainly includes money.

There are over 2,000 verses in the Bible about living the best life while fully using all available resources. There is everything from debt to budgeting to greed to work to riches to evil uses of money and everything in between. We are going to dive into many of them in this book series. But before we do, you may be asking a commonly asked question, "Why should I trust what the Bible says?"

I believe the Bible is a collection of writings recorded by everyday people and inspired by God. As you just read above in 2 Timothy 3:16, "All scripture is given by inspiration of God..." It is undoubtedly the one-hundred percent accurate, flawless Word of God. Many excellent books break down all the evidence to prove this belief. But I implore you to ask God.

Now that you have a relationship with the Almighty, you can pray, and He will answer. I will cover prayer in Chapter 4, but you need to know that God answers prayer. It may or may not be an audible answer; but you will get one—directly from God or indirectly through His word, or people.

Faith is a funny thing because it may take more faith not to believe the Word of God than to believe the Bible wholly. If you don't believe me, read the book *I Don't Have Enough Faith to Be an Atheist* by Geisler and Turek. They argue Christianity requires the least faith of all worldviews because it is the most reasonable proposition.[3]

And I have good news for you: it doesn't take a lot of faith to apply the Bible to your life. Jesus says in Matthew 17:20 that even if you have faith the size of a mustard seed, nothing will be impossible for you. I believe He uses the analogy of a mustard seed because it is such a tiny seed, yet it grows into a mighty tree.

As for evidence of the Bible's inspiration and soundness, CompellingTruth.org presents four main points. Here is a summary, but it would be worth your time to read the entire article:

1. *Fulfilled prophecy offers evidence to support God's inspiration of Scripture.*

2. *The unity of the Bible is proof of its inspiration. Do you notice how the tree of life in the last chapter of Revelation reflects the same tree in the first chapter of Genesis?*

3. *Many historical and archaeological findings support Scripture's accuracy and reliability, offering additional proof of the Bible's inspiration.*

4. *The Bible speaks accurately regarding many areas of science long before so-called discoveries.*[4]

I want to drive this point home because the financial truths explored in this book are scripturally based. And because these truths have been established as fundamental, that is further proof of the Bible's validity. I have applied these principles in my life, and the results are astonishing.

You see, when I was in my twenties, I tried to start several businesses without consulting the Great Entrepreneur, and I found myself bankrupt. In my thirties, I tried to fill voids in my life by buying experiences and stuff, but I found myself completely unsatisfied. Finally, after turning my life entirely over to Jesus, including the financial aspects, I found grace, success, and genuine freedom.

The Bible talks about all the financial management topics you could ever need. In fact, Jesus mentions money more than love and more than He spoke of heaven and hell combined. He knows you need His wisdom to manage His wealth.

Ron Blue, in writing about these principles found in the Word of God, puts it this way: "There's a huge difference between wisdom and knowledge. Knowledge simply refers to the amount of information stored in our heads, whereas wisdom refers to the framework from which we make decisions...Biblical wisdom is particularly powerful because it's transcendent and timeless. We can be confident in it because it's always right, it's always relevant, and it will never change...Principles are based on wisdom, and they're unchanging. They can be applied to anybody in any situation and still be true. They give us confidence in

I can depend

on the Holy Spirit

to bring to mind

something that

I know I should know

at just the right time.

our decisions, and they give us peace, no matter the outcome."[5]

I could write an entire book on the magnificence of the Bible, but I want to implore you to go read, research, and receive for yourself.

So, I'll end this section with this one last thought: If you ever end up in a financial situation that seems hopeless, why not turn to the Word of God? The Bible says, "For whatsoever things were written aforetime were written for our learning, **that we through patience and comfort of the scriptures might have hope**" (Romans 15:4).

Listening to the Holy Spirit

When you display your love for God, you obey His Word, but you also must abide by the promptings of His Spirit. Christ has sent us the Holy Spirit to live in us and help us. One way we have more clarity and wisdom when dealing with life's resources is through the voice of the Holy Spirit.

Some people get all spooked when discussing the Third Person of the trinity; but not you. He is there for you to speak into every situation you face. This includes financial decisions. I can testify that the Holy Spirit has saved me a ton of money as well as pain and heartache.

There are many ways to describe The Holy Spirit. But I want to explore five attributes that reveal how He keeps you on the right track financially.

Comforter—As the Comforter, the Holy Spirit gives you a sense of calm amid any financial crisis. During this year of the Covid-19 pandemic, I have heard people say that this has been an awful year. These are the same people who have not experienced any loss of life in their family. They have not had any damage to their property or possessions. They haven't even lost their job! They just chose to allow panic to come in because they were ignorant of the solution.

Our Father has a solution for all of us, and His name is the Holy Spirit.

Intercessor—The first thing I do when in need of help is to pray. That should be a given. But did you know that the Holy Spirit not only helps you pray but intercedes on your behalf? "But **the Spirit itself maketh intercession for us** with groanings which cannot be uttered" (Romans 8:26b).

Sometimes, you don't even know what to pray for or how to lay your request before the Lord. Never fear, the Holy Spirit is here. Intercession is the act of intervening on behalf of someone. And boy, do I need a lot of that!

Counselor—There is no coach like the Holy Spirit. He guides you to make the right decision when you come to a crossroads. Sometimes, I must make a split-second decision even after much prayer, and as a counselor, the Spirit can help me at just the right moment.

Jesus, referring to the Holy Spirit, said: "**He shall teach you all things**, and bring all things to your remembrance, whatsoever I have said unto you" (John 14:26b).

I love this because, while my brain is like a sieve, I can depend on the Holy Spirit to bring to mind something that I know I should know at just the right time.

The Holy Spirit also warns me lest I make the wrong decisions. I remember being presented with a business opportunity that on the surface seemed promising. But after a quick prayer, the Holy Spirit gave me wisdom in the moment, to see the problems that were not at first apparent. I could rely on the Counselor's prompting and avoid a dangerous path that would have cost me plenty.

Spirit of Revelation—Other times, you may not even know what you don't know. The Holy Spirit has given me a revelation about who to help, where to go, and what to do when I had no plan to do such things. "But God hath revealed them unto us by his Spirit: for **the Spirit searcheth all things**, yea, the deep things of God" (1 Corinthians 2:10).

Have you ever heard someone say that they just had a gut feeling? Well, you must be aware of where that feeling came from to trust it. When you see it was the Holy Spirit, don't hesitate to act on it.

Spirit of Reproof—There is another feeling that I get, which comes from the Holy Spirit, and it's called a reproof. Today we don't use this word. Its definition is similar to the words "rebuke" or "reprimand."

Speaking about the Holy Spirit, Jesus said, "And when he is come, **he will reprove the world of sin**, and of righteousness, and of judgment" (John 16:8).

And King Solomon wrote: "He that refuseth instruction despiseth his own soul: but he that heareth reproof getteth understanding" (Proverbs 15:32).

There is a much higher chance that these feelings came from the Spirit than some of my own "revelations" because I rarely tell myself "No" of my own volition. These warnings can be critical to financial success because they keep you from falling for scams and entering into dangerous deals.

To keep these magnificent attributes in front of you, download the **Financial Guidance from the Holy Spirit** infographic at the book's resource webpage: intersection.zeroinfinancial.com.[6] You can print it for reference when you need it.

Isn't the Holy Spirit awesome? And when you submit yourself to God, the Father, Son, and Holy Spirit, they are there to guide you through every situation and aspect of life.

Realize Real Financial Freedom

What is real financial freedom? Is it having a ton of money? Or is it not having to work? Or is it having the ability to do whatever you want to do, whenever you want to do it? I'm sure if I asked 100 people, I would get 100 different answers.

Sources and opinions have various definitions of freedom. One says, "Ability to make one's own choice." Another declares, "Absence of subjection to foreign domination." And a third says, "The state of not being imprisoned or enslaved."

Of all these definitions, I love the way Jesus describes the freedom He offers.

> *Are you tired? Worn out? Burned out on religion? Come to me. Get away with me and you'll recover your life. I'll show you how to take a real rest. Walk with me and work with me—watch how I do it. Learn the unforced rhythms of grace. I won't lay anything heavy or ill-fitting on you. Keep company with me and you'll learn to live freely and lightly (Matthew 11:28-30 MSG).*

Now that's the way I want to live.

I want to give you four ways I know I am living life financially free. And if you apply these principles, you can experience the very same liberty. Oh, by the way, freedom doesn't cost any money, so why not take it?

First, I know that the way I am making money, working, planning, investing, and so on, is being done according to God's will. For this to be a reality, you need to know that God exists. And not only that, you need to know

When you understand

who owns it all

and understand your

place as a steward,

you begin to use

God's Wealth with

God's Wisdom.

what God has called you to do. Then, once you are secure in your calling, you must act.

Don't worry, you will never finish: you will never be perfect. But you can be excellent in every word you speak, every action you take, every decision you make. And, when you are doing the best you can for God in Christ, you are free with the Holy Spirit empowering you.

Second, I know I am a slave only to Jesus. The borrower is a servant to the lender, so I need to stay away from credit. Addiction controls your thoughts and actions when they need to be focused on the will of God. So I need to stay away from things that tempt me into sin and dependence.

Idolatry is a freedom killer because your idol calls the shots. You have no choice but to be subject to the feelings that come over you, instead of logic and truth. You do not need to be subject to such "foreign domination." When you surrender all to Christ instead of the world's false gods, you have more focus, time, and resources: now that is true freedom! And all the while, God is gentle and noble, never forcing Himself on you.

Third, God's plan yields freedom, whereas the world's program does not. When you understand who owns it all and understand your place as a steward, you begin to use God's Wealth with God's Wisdom. When you have a Godly Mindset, you have "balance," and you feel free.

God's plan is not restrictive, seeing that He gives you a free will to make, use, and grow money as a good steward.

A wrong mindset can trap you. But when you realize there is freedom in the choices God has led you to, you are free.

You have the free will to ask God to impose His will on your life. In other words, by asking God to intersect His will with your life, you find genuine freedom.

Fourth, I have freedom from worry, fear, jealousy, depression, greed, envy, and materialism. When you are not concerned with having the latest stuff, there is freedom. Not worrying about the global or national economy, that is freedom. Not having any temptation to "keep up with the Jones's" is freedom!

Not living in worry or anxiety is freedom: "For **God hath not given us the spirit of fear;** but of power, and of love, and of a sound mind" (2 Timothy 1:7).

As a closing thought to understanding that financial freedom is rooted in a relationship as opposed to religion, I present to you a snippet from Randy Alcorn's book *Heaven*:

> *Nothing is more often misdiagnosed than our homesickness for Heaven. We think that what we want is sex, drugs, alcohol, a new job, a raise, a doctorate, a spouse, a large-screen television, a new car, a cabin in the woods, a condo in Hawaii. What we really want is the person we were made for, Jesus, and the place we were made for, Heaven. Nothing less can satisfy us.*[7]

Be sure to download the infographic

Financial Guidance from the Holy Spirit

intersection.zeroinfinancial.com[6]

CHAPTER THREE

You Need People

Isolation is extremely dangerous, not just physically and emotionally, but financially. I, unfortunately, saw the evidence of this all around me in 2020. Fortunately, I was not directly affected by this unprecedented time, though I had a heightened awareness of people suffering everywhere.

During the Covid-19 pandemic, there were mandated lockdowns. As a result, society turned into an ugly form of itself. The amount of drug use and other addictions, depression, loneliness, and divorce all skyrocketed. These results were no coincidence. We need each other.

The National Institutes of Health reports: "Human beings are social creatures. Our connection to others enables us to survive and thrive…Research has linked social isolation and loneliness to higher risks for a variety of physical and mental conditions: high blood pressure, heart disease, obesity, a weakened immune system, anxiety, depression, cognitive decline, Alzheimer's disease, and even death…Conversely, people who engage in meaningful, productive activities with others tend to live longer, boost their mood, and have a sense of purpose."[1]

We not only feel better, but we make better life decisions in general when we surround ourselves with healthy relationships. And this is undoubtedly a reality when making financial decisions, which I will explain shortly.

But where should you turn?

Why the Church is Imperfect but Vital

"And let us consider one another to provoke unto love and to good works: **Not forsaking the assembling of ourselves together**, as the manner of some is; but exhorting one another: and so much the more, as ye see the day approaching" (Hebrews 10:24-25).

The Bible here clearly warns us not to take for granted being with other Christians, particularly at church. Fellowship is critical for teaching, encouragement, and support.

During the year, churches were closed due to the social distancing requirements. This "precaution" has possibly been worse than the disease. We attended worship services online, and though it was great to hear the Word of God and get a fresh message that was very relevant for this time, the chat box was not an adequate substitute for in-person interaction.

Calling fellow brothers and sisters is always something we should practice regularly, but this activity should be in addition to being physically together. Social media is undoubtedly not a suitable replacement for the face-to-face contact our humanity craves. Video conferencing has become the best alternative so that we can see and hear each other; but there is nothing like a hug, holding hands, and being near that smile or tear.

When life opens back up after these restrictions, will this phase be a wake-up call? Will relationships become a higher priority? Will people realize that they are better together? You are reading this after the fact, so you should be able to look around and see if there are any visible after-effects on our community.

I've heard many reasons for someone deciding not to attend church. Although there may be some valid concerns, that is not a reason to avoid congregating. I have news for you: the church is not perfect. And because it is full of imperfect people, you will fit right in. Not going to church, for this reason, would be like saying, "I am not going to the hospital because there are sick people there."

Christianity is all about relationships, and as with all relationships, you need to nurture and grow them.

Remember that the church is not a building but a body of people. We Christians are all sinners washed by the blood of Jesus, and therefore, born again. But the flesh still co-exists. You still have habits you need to break, temptations you must resist, and truths you must discover.

So Christianity is all about relationships, and as with all relationships, you need to nurture and grow them. Marriage has its challenges, no matter how long ago you said, "I do." The same goes for your Christian walk. You need to give yourself grace, but you need to offer those at church grace even more so.

Don't forsake assembling with fellow believers. If you ignore this directive, you will miss out on helping that single mom who needs someone to sit down with her and walk through a budget together. When you are not at church, you won't have the opportunity to impact that young person's life in their battle with a financially dysfunctional home. Not being in a church means not having the chance to go down to the altar and have that older and wiser gentleman lay hands on you as he prays for your income dilemma.

Like a flower, it takes work to cultivate meaningful relationships, but the beauty of the bloom far exceeds the sacrifice. I admit, I'm guilty myself of not nurturing the plant, while expecting it to grow.

It was a wake-up call for me to think about how I didn't have a relationship with anyone in my church when not at church. We would see each other on Sunday, say hello and goodbye, and that was it. If I went out of town, or I missed a couple services, I wouldn't get a phone call. When brothers and sister who I serve with every week were not at their usual posts, I didn't seek to find out how they were doing either.

The reason we didn't seem to care is because we had no relationship outside of the walls of the church building, for the most part. We were more like acquaintances, not friends, let alone "brother" or "sister." Sometimes, I wouldn't even notice their absence until the next Sunday when I would see them the next time. That's when we would say, "Oh, I missed you, brother. Where have you been?"

When there's no relationship outside of church with the people you go to church with, you don't get to develop those relationships beyond "hello" and "bye bye." You may pray together and worship together, but you don't really get to know them at a deeper level. They won't be there for you when you need them because they don't get to know you outside of Sunday morning.

Just like any loving parent, God wants His children to be close and to support each other even after the Sunday morning service's final Amen. We need each other for accountability and advice. During grieving and laughter. To play games with and grow up together. To celebrate with and, of course, pray through every situation, including financial. And church is where these deep meaningful relationships begin.

You Need an Accountability Partner

When traversing the intricacies of finances, you also need an accountability partner. They should be someone at the level of or beyond where you are in the arena of money management and financial astuteness. You don't want someone who is a shopaholic or considering bankruptcy to be your accountability partner. Choose someone who can speak into your life, someone you respect.

An accountability partner is even more critical for someone who is not married. Single-people, do not avoid finding this important person in your life. The person you choose should be someone with the heart of a teacher, yes, compassionate, but not afraid to tell you the truth. You know you can let your emotions get the better of you as well. If you don't have someone like this already in your life, an excellent financial coach will fill the void.

If you are married, you already have an accountability partner in your spouse. You are going to have some tough conversations. There will be times of simple decisions and other times when you must compromise. But you cannot afford not to have this foundational piece in place; so, if your spouse does not want to get involved, ask him or her to try it out with you for 90 days. When people see they are ultimately going to enjoy money more, their hesitation dissipates.

As someone married, there is a temptation to do this financial stuff alone if you have a reluctant or distant spouse. If this is the case, I would suggest that you get in touch with your pastor or good marriage counselor and work on your marriage. If your spouse doesn't want to go to a counselor, do it alone to get advice. It is more important to get your marriage on the right track than your common financial dreams in sync. The latter will fall into place once you confront the former.

In fact, many couples say that, after doing the budget together month after month, their marriage has improved. That makes sense. The number one reason for divorce is communication about money matters. So, if you agree on the budget before a dime leaves your bank account, there are no money fights. Of course, this only happens if you stick to the plan. A blueprint is no good if you do not follow it. The same principle applies to a budget.

You should consider an accountability partner even if you are married, or even better, an accountability couple! When you have a wiser (and many times older) couple who come alongside you, your marriage will be all the better. They will have a vantage point to see things the two of you cannot see. They will be there to pray with you, tell you stories of their experience, and give you a perspective that may develop your lives in more ways than managing wealth. I promise, if you employ this strategy, blessings will follow.

I've saved an entire chapter to do a thorough analysis into the subject of prayer, but as I mentioned above, your accountability partner should be a person (or couple) who is a prayer partner. Where human advice falls short, prayer goes the distance. "Confess your faults one to another, and pray one for another, that ye may be healed. **The effectual fervent prayer of a righteous man availeth much**" (James 5:16).

And since you are comfortable discussing these confidential financial matters with someone you are accountable to, they will know just how to pray.

I praise God that He has always provided me and Christine with incredible accountability partners for personal finances and business strategy alike. If you are in business for yourself, you must find a person with whom you can mutually invest in by this means. Even while crafting this book, I have a writing accountability partner who I meet with every week to discuss issues, discover solutions, celebrate wins, and pray all the way. I hugely appreciate and love him dearly.

Surround Yourself with Likeminded People

Jim Rohn famously said: "You're the average of the five people you spend the most time with." So, if your five closest friends are all broke and have no reverence for God, you might need new friends.

I'm joking (kind of), but you need to be careful who influences your everyday thinking and actions. If you surround yourself with people who are always worried, you most likely will be afraid of everything. But if those in your inner circle are all motivated, joyful, and blessed individuals, it will be contagious.

When I've observed people who have no wisdom with finances, I notice that the closest people in their life are the same. I have acquaintances who swear by their credit card points, and when I dig into how they began down this path, I find out that their friends got them started. The same goes for high-risk investments, like cryptocurrencies. I don't know anyone who invests in Bitcoin, Dogecoin, or Dai who doesn't have buddies who do the same. If fear grips their strategy as evidenced by their nest egg being tied up in CDs and annuities, there are surely several people in their life who have nurtured these unstable emotions.

But guess what? The opposite is even more real. I surround myself with others who know that God owns everything, and we are managers. My closest friend's financial strategies are guided by Biblical principles. My advisors, mentors, and coaches understand that working hard, getting rich slowly, and giving most of it away is essential for financial freedom. The result: I am financially full of joy and empty of anxiety.

"Then **make my joy complete by being like-minded**, having the same love, being one in spirit and of one mind. ... In your relationships with one another, **have the same mindset as Christ Jesus**" (Philippians 2:2,5 NIV).

As you will see in Chapter 5, worry is a sin. But I also want to tell you here that worry is contagious. If you surround yourself with people who are watching the stock market every minute and reacting to its ups and downs, you will lose your mind with fear. Watch the news every day for three hours, and you will be in the doctor's office being prescribed pills to calm your nerves.

If your enemy, the devil, can isolate you and keep you in a state of doubt and fear, you're done. Instead of positioning yourself amongst Christian brothers and sisters who can encourage, support and love you, you find yourself struggling, weak, and eventually desperate. This is when you make unwise financial moves, putting yourself right where the enemy wants you.

Trust God because He's got this! And then, surround yourself with level-headed, logical thinking brothers and sisters in the Lord. Like I said before, the church is full of imperfect people, so don't choose just anyone to be your closest confidants.

You can spot the best people for fellowship a mile away. First, they seem to be happy all the time (now that's a rare sight!). Second, they speak words of life, words that encourage and energize you. Third, you never see them gossip or put someone down, even when the opportunity presents itself.

One last word of warning: you may run into people who seem happy, but not because of their faith in the One who is in control. They, instead, are careless and carefree:

God will provide

all your needs

here on earth,

and He wants you to

enjoy riches here.

no plan, no discipline, and they plain don't care. You may think they have it all together, but the fact is, their joy relies on a false foundation. Be aware of people in this category; instead, pray for them, and see if you can give them some loving guidance.

Solomon writes, "Without counsel purposes are disappointed: but **in the multitude of counsellors they are established**" (Proverbs 15:22).

Relationships Lead to Riches

I notice people get hung up with an envious mindset of the kid with wealthy parents. This mindset is not healthy because jealousy and, even worse, envy, is poison to your financial plan.

Furthermore, don't you want to leave a legacy of wealth for your children's children? Because you financially plan according to the Word of God, you may become very wealthy for yourself, your family, and the good of others. How wonderful to leave a legacy of wealth and the wisdom to go along with it!

When you understand our Maker made a way through Jesus Christ for you and me to become children of the Living God, you realize how extraordinary your inheritance is. Your Father is infinitely wealthy indeed, and His Holy Spirit is our assurance. **"The Spirit is God's guarantee that he will give us the inheritance** he promised and that he has purchased us to be his own people. He did this so we would praise and glorify him" (Ephesians 1:14 NLT).

Of course, some may argue that our inheritance is stored in heaven to enjoy when we pass from this world. But I'm here to tell you that Scripture says that God will provide all your needs here on earth, and He wants you to enjoy riches here. "Charge them that are rich in this world, that they be not high-minded, nor trust in uncertain riches, but in **the living God, who giveth us richly all things to enjoy**" (1 Timothy 6:17).

Your relationship with God leads to riches here on earth. These riches get passed on, whether you like it or not. While you are alive, you get to give via relationships of charity, familial relationships, through mentoring, and beyond. Then, after you die, your last wishes are carried out.

When you have no healthy relationships, wealth turns into "uncertain riches." You may have money, you may pass on assets, you may even get wealth from an inheritance; but it is not a blessing. I've seen money fights between siblings because of improperly executed legacies. Relationships become strained because someone didn't give enough in the other person's eyes. Money causes pain when it is not blessed.

Remember, "The blessing of the Lord, it maketh rich, and **he addeth no sorrow with it**" (Proverbs 10:22). If you have strained relationships because of financial misunderstandings, you need to bring the circumstance to the Lord. Pray and ask God if you need to do anything differently. Seek to guide the other party into a right relationship with Jesus. Find Godly counsel together.

Life is too short to have money disputes. Prayerful planning can preserve relationships, and the lack of a plan can ruin them. In fact, if you dig deeper, you find that money is rarely the actual issue. When you find healing in your interactions, you will realize the riches are in the relationships, not the finances.

Prosperity resides where prayerful planning, financial freedom, and radical relationships intersect.

In closing out this first part of the book, I would like to encourage you to study and meditate on these three verses:

"Behold, how good and how pleasant it is for brethren to dwell together in unity!" (Psalm 133:1)

"Greater love hath no man than this, that a man lay down his life for his friends" (John 15:13).

"Iron sharpeneth iron; so a man sharpeneth the countenance of his friend" (Proverbs 27:17).

Part II

Faith Meets Strategy

CHAPTER FOUR

Pray First

Check out this scripture: "Don't worry about anything; instead, **pray about everything. Tell God what you need and thank him for all he has done.** Then you will experience God's peace, which exceeds anything we can understand. His peace will guard your hearts and minds as you live in Christ Jesus" (Philippians 4:6-7 NLT).

Don't miss the last six words of this scripture: "…as you live in Christ Jesus." Real financial success is realized as you live a life dedicated to the One who gave you everything. If you missed it, Chapter 1 tells you why and how to live in Jesus. Do that first. Then, as you prayerfully

Real financial success

is realized

as you live a life

dedicated to

the One who gave you

everything.

plan, ask Jesus what He would have you do with the resources He has provided.

God doesn't want anyone to be anxious. It is never His will for you to worry. But have you worried about something concerning your financial position in the last year? The last month? Week? Day?

As I've listened to the news (which I try not to) or spoken to clients, friends, or family over the past year, I always sense a tinge of worry. Many people are concerned about the economy. They are worried about what a family member might do or think about their possessions. The possibility of a job loss is at the back of their mind. The list goes on and on.

But the Bible says not to worry about anything. Some may worry about just a few things, but that is not how we should live. Instead, give *all* your fears and anxiety over to Jesus.

The media is trying to push the idea that you should be gravely concerned with all things, all of the time. Of course, this is the best way to keep you glued to their programming, bringing them colossal advertising dollars. They are not dumb, and they know just what to do to bring in the most profit.

The problem is that this idea is the direct opposite of what the Word of God says. Imagine a life with no worries ever about anything! That's what God wants for your life.

A worry-free life may seem impossible, especially if you only know one way of living. But I would like to present to you a principle that comes with no anxiety about finances.

The answer is obvious, "...instead, pray about everything." Yep, it's that easy.

Resorting to Prayer

The word "resort" is often preceded by the adjective "last." I hear people talk about their last resort when they are on the verge of giving up. And too many times, that last resort is prayer.

I know this phrase is not proper English, but you should make prayer your "first resort"! Whether you are full or empty, resort to prayer before anything else. That is what I hope for every individual to practice daily in every aspect of their lives.

As I help people with their relationship with money, I never forget who owns it all. When budgeting, it is easy to begin by diving right into the numbers, especially for a nerd like me.

Instead, I've learned that you must first give thanks to God, our Provider, no matter how much or little you have to manage. Then lay all your needs and desires before Him.

This principle of financial success is certainly not a secret. It's been written, printed, spoken about, and widely available for thousands of years. And prayer is the ground where real financial success is rooted.

In Philippians 4:6-7, you will find the first step: "Tell God what you need." Have you laid before God all your needs? I mean all: the good, the bad, and the ugly?

Eleven years ago, I found myself at the beginning of what I now know was the process of digging an enormous hole. I thought I knew what I was doing. But, looking back, I see I was making every financial decision without prayer. The result? Over $100,000 of debt and a ton of worry.

God is our loving Father. He cares about everything you need, just like every loving parent does. But here's the difference: He creates all things and owns all things, unlike our earthly parents. Learn more about ownership in *God's Ownership Meets Money Management.*

Do you see what I see? He can provide anything, anytime, anywhere, simply because He is God. And He loves you so much that He is just waiting for you to come to Him with your request.

Before dedicating my life to be a financial teacher and coach, I was studying to be a wealth advisor. And en route to passing the Series 7 and Series 66 exams, I had to memorize this quote: "Past performance is not indicative of future results." You may have heard this before on financial product commercials or in the fine print of an investment firm's advertisements.

On the other hand, investing in prayer is just the opposite because God is the same yesterday, today, and forever. God's past performance IS CERTAINLY indicative of future results!

The next step is to thank Him: "... and thank Him for all He has done."

There is nothing worse than seeing your kid get handed a gift from someone, and they do not say, "Thank you." You know how it is. We lean over and whisper to our child: "What do you say?" Don't be that kid!

We should wake up thanking God for the roof over our heads, the food in the fridge, the clothes on our backs, and so much more. That is just the tip of the iceberg as far as the goodness He has provided.

What about the ability to work and earn a living? Sanity and intelligence? Friends and family? Believe me, if you don't think God has given you these things, test Him—no, please, don't do that!

God created you; He loves you; He wants the best for you. Just ask, and He will provide.

The Quick Fix

I have a confession. When I have a headache, I tend to go for the medicine cabinet, miserably searching for my drug of choice to soothe the pain. The bottle says that it will take care of the problem in 30 minutes or less. There is nothing wrong with taking medicine. But I have come to realize that I have made taking the drug my priority. I want a quick fix.

In every situation, I want solutions as fast as possible, especially when it's just a random and seemingly small obstacle. For example, my debit card was declined at the store, and I knew the money was there. So, I feel my anxiety rising as I think of what and who to blame. I exclaim to the cashier that surely he was doing something wrong, only to get a response of doubt in my ability to pay. "Call your bank," he calmly replies.

Walking away very unchristian like, I'm thinking about how this has derailed my schedule. Now comes the peak of frustration as I negotiate my way through my bank help line's phone tree only to reach elevator music five minutes later. Being on hold is the worst! I want this done now. Why is this taking so long? Shouldn't there be a quick fix?

I never prayed. God was the last one on my mind. In contrast, the Bible instructs us to ask God first. When I finally tossed up a Hail Mary request for help, God still answered because He loves me.

It amazes me how patient God is; how much He cares for us, and how He loves us unconditionally. No, we don't deserve an ounce of His mercy and grace, but He is faithful to gives it to us. All the same, He is not a "quick fix" God. He may let us wait a little while—for our own good.

If I had calmly asked God to help me when the issue arose, I may have been through the cashier line in three minutes instead of thirty. I may have even seen the alert from my bank's app asking if I wanted to authorize the transaction that was over my daily limit (the one I set up months ago and forgot about).

Relying on God

for all things,

all the time,

first and foremost

will save you tons of

time, stress, and

money.

There was another time long ago when I was trying to fix the lawnmower myself, with little luck. Then I began searching on the Internet for help, getting progressively frustrated. Finally, I went to Home Depot to ask the "experts," who all gave me a look of bewilderment. I then threw up my hands and said, "I guess all I have left to do is pray."

The lawnmower starts.

Relying on God for all things, all the time, first and foremost will save you tons of time, stress, and money. We have good intentions in our methods to find remedies in life, but many times, we do things in the wrong order. Too often, we gravitate towards the quick fix.

I notice I tend to ask no one for help first. Trying to figure stuff out on my own is important to me. This is very prideful, which is the arch enemy of reliance on God the Provider. My real wake-up call was realizing that I put prayer last, even though I know that, after I pray, the plan goes so much more smoothly. I now see the power of making prayer the first resort, not the last.

God loves you and wants the best for you, so when you come to Him with your request, you can count on Him to give you the perfect prescription. Though His remedy is not always what you'd expect, His will for your life is better than what you may desire. It may not be a quick fix, but it will be the best fix.

It was a huge lesson for me to learn that the quick fix is not always healthy. This is obvious in curing physical ailments. The fastest working drugs always come with a laundry list of side effects. Sometimes the results of these quick fixes are worse than the initial condition.

The same happens many times when there are financial predicaments and obstacles in life. I've coached people who have prayed for money that they thought they desperately needed immediately. It didn't come right away, though. Instead, it took months of contending in prayer for it to be answered.

Looking back, they thank God for that period of time because they came out of it on the other side healthier, smarter, stronger, and more financially fit than ever before in their life. It's funny how we end up thanking God for not allowing the quick fix to come to fruition.

"**Pray without ceasing**. In everything give thanks: for this is the will of God in Christ Jesus concerning you" (1 Thessalonians 5:17-18).

Waiting

In the same way the sun never grows weary of shining, nor a stream of flowing, it is God's nature to keep His promises (Charles Spurgeon).

I know well that my timing is not God's timing. I am not very patient, while God is extraordinarily patient. Waiting is hard, but it is a muscle that can be made strong. It is always best to wait upon the Lord.

As a dad, I always think about the answers I gave my kids when they were young. God created us in His image; therefore, I believe our loving Father put those answers in us. As a dad, my three go-to answers were yes, no, and wait!

Oh no, God could say, "Wait?" Yes, He can, and He does. This realization completely changed my expectation for immediate resolutions. But, just like my kids would ask me, I many times ask God, "Why?"

I love my children, and I would only have them wait if there was a reason that not waiting would not be best. For example, when a child pulls your hand to go, they may not notice the bike coming down the sidewalk across your path. You say "Wait" to protect them.

Other times, you tell your child to wait so that they learn to build up that patience muscle. I've seen that dad with his son coaching him at the baseball diamond. He says, "Don't swing too early. Get a good look at the pitch. Wait till just the right moment." But then, the kid flails away far in front of the ball because he couldn't wait. The professionals do it, too (as a batting coach somewhere sighs).

"For since the world began, no ear has heard and no eye has seen a God like you, who works for those who wait for him!" (Isaiah 64:4 NLT)

And so we get anxious, and we decide to get ahead of God. I've done it with employment, investing, spending, and, yeah, pretty much every area of finance. Learning how to wait can save you lots of money.

In the introduction of his book *A Tithe of Time*, William Jordan states: "Christians today tend to be too busy and too stressed. We have lost the patience to 'be still and know that (He is) God' (Psalm 46:10). The result of our busy, stressful way of life is that most Christians struggle to hear the 'still small voice' of the Lord."

Jordan continues, "We are desperate to know God's will and purpose for our life, and we complain that God doesn't speak to us; yet we Christians often give God a little time on Sundays and not much else."[1]

But what are we supposed to do while waiting? Well, this is where relationship trumps religion. As I discussed in Chapter 2, God loves you so much that He wants to commune with you.

The Lord wants to spend time with you, hear about your feelings, and listen to your requests. But He also longs for you to worship Him and thank Him for all He has done for you. Giving Him a little time only on Sunday doesn't sound like much of a relationship.

We have so many reasons to be thankful. I don't know about other countries, but here in America, we are so blessed; yet we have gotten so spoiled. Take time, in the waiting, to give your Lord and Provider thanks.

What if you only called your mother on Christmas and Easter? How would that make her feel? Would she feel loved? But that's often how we treat God.

If you only came home to your spouse on Sundays, your marriage would suffer. You could say, "He knows I love him," but I'm reasonably sure that most people could see your actions are not matching your words. However, I see this scenario play out for churchgoers all the time.

And as you are waiting, use this time to study His Word. You might even find the answer to your concerns there. Don't leave out scripture memorization. For, we can forget so much of the Bible even if we regularly read it. It will help you along your Christian walk to have verses committed to memory and deep within your heart.

Here is a verse you should memorize today if you have not: "But they that **wait upon the Lord** shall renew their strength; they shall mount up with wings as eagles; they shall run, and not be weary; and they shall walk, and not faint" (Isaiah 40:31).

The website, Knowing-Jesus.com, gives some wisdom regarding this verse. One part of it says, "It is faith in His word that is needed to soar with wings as eagles. It is trusting God to bring to pass all He has promised, even when our senses and logic seem to suggest the opposite or appear to contradict His promised truth. Those who wait on the Lord are those who have the assurance and inner confidence that the promises He has made to His people, and the things for which we hope, are a matter of fact and a present reality...that cannot be contradicted by senses, emotions, reason or fear."[2]

After prayerfully planning, whether it is your monthly budget, your estate plan, your five-year financial forecast, your business's balance sheet, etc., set it aside for a period.

During that time of waiting, pray about it, meditate on God's Word, and let God speak to you.

As you "mount up with wings as eagles," you can visualize the plan and the solutions through a different lens and from a fresh vantage point. When you see your dreams on the other side of waiting, you will see them significantly improved.

The Most Important Financial Target

When I rebranded and rebooted my coaching business, I made it a point to have a clear and specific mission. I knew those whom I serve needed to accomplish four objectives:

1. *RECOVER from past money mistakes,*
2. *GROW their present pocketbook position,*
3. *ZERO IN on their future financial fortune,*
4. *ultimately leaving a lasting legacy of love.*

All these happen simultaneously and continuously, but not instantaneously. I then realized that my clients would naturally RECOVER and GROW as I pray with them and helped them ZERO IN! Thus, Zero In Financial® was born.

Everyone is building their own unique financial house. The kitchen is wafting with smells of delicious food to sustain your household. There may be a room for kids' toys and a living room full of books helping them grow up strong with knowledge and understanding of work and play. The walls are covered with memories. The recreation space is full of entertainment, relaxation, and renewal.

There are ever-expanding additions of charity and support for all the people and organizations God has laid upon your heart. Your financial house has a strong roof with the shingles of retirement and asset protection. The floors are sturdy with assurance for the future. There is a hedge of protection that surrounds the perimeter of the property. Legacy planning is locked away, secure in the family safe. God has a plan for you to prosper and pass on much knowledge and wealth.

It is your financial house.

But your financial house needs a sound foundation, and that is what this book series is all about. Every foundation begins with a survey to ensure you are building at the best site. That location would be at the intersection of God's Wealth and God's Wisdom for your life and purpose.

So, in summary, to build your dream financial house, you must first lay a solid foundation. You can find the best place to form that foundation by first surveying the land. And your survey must begin by zeroing in.

You may be asking the question I hope you are asking, "Zero in on what?" And that is why I named my blog post page *Zero In On This*. Find the ever-growing library of articles written to guide you as you zero in on your financial target here: blog.zeroinfinancial.com.[3]

I asked God to help me determine the most crucial aspect of finances He would have me help people zero in on. Like a surveyor, you must have a target to aim at before zeroing in your sights. So, you will find the blog site divided up into different categories (targets), each founded on a key scripture for the Word of God. I hope you find each article's guidance intriguing, and I would love suggestions for future writing.

I'm sure you won't be surprised to find that the most crucial target to zero in on is to Prayerfully Plan. It should always be the first resort. Pray with a purpose to praise, thank, and obey. And be sure that answered prayers lie at the intersection of your request and God's will for your life.

You may not even know what to pray for, but pray nonetheless for God to find a solution. While you are praying and hoping and wishing for a door to be opened, God is working on your behalf. All the while you are praying for a specific door to be open, God may be preparing for you a door you don't even see.

Think about that: there may be a door that you don't even know exists. If you knew this door existed, you would pray for that door to be opened. So, all the while you're wondering and wishing and hoping and complaining about a financial or other situation, God is preparing for you a better door, a better path, a better way that you don't even know exists.

So, when that door is revealed, you will see the will of God and all that He has for you that you didn't even know to pray for. Stop praying for a door to be opened. And stop wondering why a particular way has not been made clear. But start praying for *the* door to be opened; the one that God desires for you to enter; the one you may not even be aware of. Remember from Chapter 1, God's ways are not our ways.

You will learn more about these targets as you explore this book series and subsequent writings. But you can also go to the Zero In Financial Blog and find articles categorized by each target. Also, by subscribing, you will get a notification when new helpful articles are published. Check it all out at: blog.zeroinfinancial.com.[3]

CHAPTER FIVE

Don't Worry

Remember that song, *Don't Worry; Be Happy?* Well, God came up with those words thousands of years before Bobby McFerrin was even born. Your Heavenly Father, the Maker and Owner of everything, is faithful. So, it doesn't do much good to worry.

Read what Jesus said in the book of Matthew:

> *Therefore I say unto you, Take no thought for your*
> *life, what ye shall eat, or what ye shall drink; nor*
> *yet for your body, what ye shall put on. Is not the*
> *life more than meat, and the body than raiment?*

Behold the fowls of the air: for they sow not, neither do they reap, nor gather into barns; yet your heavenly Father feedeth them.

Are ye not much better than they? Which of you by taking thought can add one cubit unto his stature? And why take ye thought for raiment? Consider the lilies of the field, how they grow; they toil not, neither do they spin: And yet I say unto you, That even Solomon in all his glory was not arrayed like one of these. Wherefore, if God so clothe the grass of the field, which to day is, and to morrow is cast into the oven, shall he not much more clothe you, O ye of little faith?

Therefore take no thought, saying, What shall we eat? or, What shall we drink? or, Wherewithal shall we be clothed? (For after all these things do the Gentiles seek:) for your heavenly Father knoweth that ye have need of all these things. But seek ye first the kingdom of God, and his righteousness; and all these things shall be added unto you. Take therefore no thought for the morrow: for the morrow shall take thought for the things of itself. Sufficient unto the day is the evil thereof (Matthew 6:25-34).

Just think about how those emergencies will feel when you are not worried. You have a completely transformed perspective when you expect things to happen in life, and you have nothing to fear. Your outlook is entirely different after you put the proper defenses in place. Your financial foundation is strong.

You may get into an accident or have a house fire. Your landlord's building has a flood, and your stuff is in the basement. You plonk yourself down on a rock-hard park bench and realize your $1000 phone is in your back pocket. Someone may die or get a severe illness. In all of these situations, I know it will be tough. But you won't be stressed out financially.

Worry dissipates with proper prayer, proper planning, and proper protection. Now that you have prayed first, it is time to plan and protect God's wealth according to Godly wisdom.

Worry is a sin because it directly opposes faith. The more worry, the less faith you have, and the further away from the intersection you will drift.

Pastor Chuck Swindoll preached in his sermon *The Subtle Enemy of Simple Faith*, "Worry is assuming responsibility for things that are out of our control. That's pretty much everything."[1] You only worry when you either don't think God can, or you don't think He cares. Neither is ever true.

You learned the remedy at the beginning of the last chapter: "**Don't worry about anything**; instead, pray about everything" (Philippians 4:6a NLT). So now let's put these verses into action.

Worry dissipates with proper prayer, proper planning, and proper protection.

Proper Planning

While our church was in a building project, my pastor taught that when planning God's way, it takes part faith and part strategy. And I often see people miss their target when considering one without the other.

If you plan with faith and no strategy, you will pray and pray all the while God is waiting for you to get up and start moving. In contrast, approaching the plan without faith is self-centered instead of God-centered, resulting in arriving at the wrong destination.

In her timeless book *What the Bible is All About*, Henrietta Mears says, "There is one thing to do always: Do what is right and leave the rest to God. God prepares people for emergencies. Failure is not sin; faithlessness is."[2]

We need a healthy balance of faith and strategy. While a 50:50 split seems like it will work, a balanced ratio looks more like 1:99. We take one step of faithful obedience for every 99 steps taken by God. It doesn't seem fair, but God does most of the work by far.

To see how faith relates to money, we can look to all that was written about the father of our faith, Abraham, who was blessed beyond belief.

> For the Scriptures tell us, "Abraham believed God, and God counted him as righteous because of his faith."

When people work, their wages are not a gift, but something they have earned. But people are counted as righteous, not because of their work, but because of their faith in God who forgives sinners.

Clearly, God's promise to give the whole earth to Abraham and his descendants was based not on his obedience to God's law, but on a right relationship with God that comes by faith.

So the promise is received by faith. It is given as a free gift. And we are all certain to receive it, whether or not we live according to the law of Moses, if we have faith like Abraham's. For Abraham is the father of all who believe (Romans 4:3-5,13,16 NLT).

Today, the word "faith" has been abused. Everyone says they have faith. But you must ask "Faith in who?" to get to the source of their faith. We know that the only faith that will firm up your financial foundation is the faith that results in a right relationship with Jesus Christ. This is the reason you must begin with the principles I presented in Part I of this book.

God promised to give the whole earth as an inheritance to Abraham and his descendants, who are you and me. The whole earth? Yes. God owns everything, and He gives each of us a portion to manage. But to manage it well, we must have faith like Abraham, faith in the One who made it all. And we, unlike Abraham, have continuous access to the Owner of Everything by accepting His free gift of salvation through Jesus, the Son of God.

Paul writes to the Galatians: "And now that you belong to Christ, you are the true children of Abraham. You are his heirs, and **God's promise to Abraham belongs to you**" (Galatians 3:29 NLT).

Oh, by the way, Abraham honored God with all his resources, energy, and time; in other words, he managed God's Wealth with God's Wisdom. Because of his relationship, he was obedient to the will of God. And because he yielded to the Spirit, he realized the great potential God had in store for him.

The result? Most experts agree he would be a Multi-Billionaire in today's U.S. dollars. This resulted from being blessed by God. Not because of greed. Nor materialism. There was no self-centered motivation. Only trust in the Master Financial Planner.

So, when I pray through all my plans, I like to pray first, plan second, and then pray to the finish line. Remember that all great goals, including financial objectives, get tested. So, if you are not prayed-up, these tests can topple your plan.

Part of planning how to handle wealth is planning your time. As I mentioned in previous chapters, set aside a dedicated time to pray and read your Bible. You must also set aside time for a monthly budget meeting and weekly financial reconciliation. During this time, God will give you wisdom as you plan how to manage His wealth.

Having a budget is essential for a healthy financial plan. It shocks me to learn how many Christians faithfully budget, while not earnestly praying about these figures first. They copy and paste, tweaking numbers how they see fit, but never consult the One who provided the numbers. Of course, later, they wonder why it didn't work out as expected.

There are many things to plan for, and I won't cover all of them here, but this faith-strategy principle has application in each. For example, choosing a university, buying a house, and solidifying your estate plan are all particularly expensive. The key to being worry-free is having faith in God, asking Him for guidance, and knowing that the strategy is not yours alone.

I want to pose a question to anyone who says that they have faith: Does faith have you? Pastor D. Greg Ebie writes in his book series *Resurrected Faith* about faith originating as a verb. Once faith has you, you live what you believe; the activity of faith affects everything you do, including planning. He says, "Consider this like the software of a computer. The programming and code of this world fill our minds, but the Spirit begins the work of 'faithing' within us. In this way, **the activity of faith begins the process to transform the output of how we think, talk, and act."**[3]

Through the activity of faith, you will begin properly planning God's way, which is the best strategy.

Proper Protection

Along with planning, you must have a hedge of protection. God will protect His wealth from many internal and external risks. He also expects you to be smart and have the proper tools in place to mitigate those risks. Insurance is one of them. Remember, part strategy. Not all insurances are necessary, but some are imperative.

I won't go into all the kinds of insurance, but it is essential to think about the foundation before building for the future. As this Bible translation states: "When the storm is over, ... good people, **firm on their rock foundation**, aren't even fazed" (Proverbs 10:25 MSG).

God is the Rock, with a capital "R." Insurance is a rock, but with a lowercase "r." You need both.

Proper Protection means having several layers of defense in place. The first line of defense is being faithful in tithing. I will go into much detail about this protection in *God's Ownership Meets Money Management*. I actually spend ten percent of this series on the topic of tithing.

Another layer is having the right insurance policies in place. Now, with added insurance to your life's most relevant areas, the big stuff is secure. You now know you can deal with a catastrophic storm in your financial life. It's a great feeling to know that something terrible could happen, something genuinely life-altering, but it won't be devastating to your financial house. The worst is never easy, but it's nice to know that you are prepared to weather the storm.

Part of your security is having formed a money plan, a budget for next month, and a financial forecast for the future. It may not be precisely mathematically correct the first time you create a budget, but it will get more fine-tuned as you move along. Directing those dollars where they should go instead of wondering where they have disappeared to is so liberating. This piece keeps the foundation "true" for sure. I've found people think they don't need a budget because they don't have any financial problems. But after they see how a budget protects and preserves their wealth, they consider giving it a try.

Now that you have a budget, it's time to defend against the small stuff. The first insurance policy you need, no agency can give you. This insurance gives you peace of mind. It transforms crises into inconveniences. This type of insurance is better known as an emergency fund, rainy day fund, or even Grandma's cookie jar fund.

Life happens, and we never know when it is going to happen. I'm talking about those unexpected "emergencies." Let's transform emergencies into inconveniences by having money set aside for those moments. Insurance will handle the costly problems while the emergency fund takes care of everything else.

Often, my clients will dwell on past events that have happened to them that caused them to borrow money, or work a second job, or go into crisis mode emotionally. Life happened to them, and they were unprepared. They did not have a firm foundation in place.

The good news is that it doesn't have to be this way. You can insure against the significant events and have money set aside for the minor stuff.

Dave Ramsey, the author of *The Total Money Makeover* and host of one of the largest talk radio shows and podcasts, has the best course on personal financial management: *Financial Peace University*. In this class, you learn what he calls the Baby Steps. If you have never taken this class, I highly recommend that you do. It may be the best money you have ever spent because the return on investment is astronomical.

One expression Dave has coined is "Normal is Broke." The last thing you want to be is regular or average, in America, at least. The typical American is walking around with leaky, damaged, or non-existent financial foundations.

According to Bankrate's Financial Security Index survey, from January 2018, "More than one-third of [American] households, 34 percent, endured a major unexpected expense over the past year, ... with only 39 percent saying they would cover a $1,000 blow with savings."[4]

Wait; what?

Sixty-one percent of Americans have less than $1000 in the bank? Then, how will they deal with a minor emergency? How will they be able to pay the deductible on the insurance claim when they get into a car accident? What will happen when their house roof leaks? Where will they turn when that medical issue pops up?

Statistics reveal that a third of the population experienced one of these occurrences in the last year. Using debt was many times the answer {insert sad face}. Credit was the "solution" to each emergency, says the Bankrate article. As Dave says, "The worst time to go into debt is in the midst of an emergency," yet that is precisely what the average person does. It's time to stop this madness.

Not having an emergency fund is truly being undisciplined and irresponsible with your finances. If you want to do your part in protecting God's wealth, you need one.

I began teaching people how to Holistically Hedge because you need multiple strategies of protection against the storms of life. Prayer, planning, insuring, and emergency funding are all important components to safeguarding your assets. You've worked too hard to allow your financial house to take a beating.

This subject of protection and preservation deserves its own chapter, maybe even a book or a series. I hope to one day be able to do a deep dive into all the aspects of hedging the wealth God has entrusted to you to manage.

Until that time, read the Holistically Hedge section on my blog for tidbits of Biblical wisdom.

Proper Preparation

You can see here in this Bible passage how Joseph listened to the Lord's direction and was therefore prepared for the subsequent famine. "Have them gather all the food produced in the good years that are just ahead and bring it to Pharaoh's storehouses. Store it away, and guard it so there will be food in the cities" (Genesis 41:35 NLT).

Study this entire story of how God's plan saved many lives and provided sustenance for the entire region. It may surprise you to learn how saving for this emergency was even better than an insurance plan. This plan resulted in great riches for Joseph and the entire kingdom.

Your emergency fund can save you money on your insurance, and that savings can result in compounding wealth. As you walk through a review of your insurance, I advise you set the deductible to the highest comfortable limit. That amount should be relative to the amount of your emergency fund. It's all about preparation as God leads you.

You can't predict the future, but you can be prepared no matter your current financial state. For example, when you are still crushing debt, it is best to keep the emergency fund at $1000 and therefore, your insurance deductibles should be kept low. But once you have a fully funded emergency fund, you can set them higher, saving a lot of money over time.

This HuffPost article reports:

> *According to the National Association of Insurance Commissioners (NAIC), the average annual auto insurance premium is $841, and the study [Quadrant Information Services study, commissioned by insuranceQuotes] examined two different percentage increases and their respective savings (on average): Increase deductible from $500 to $1,000: 9 percent savings ($72). Increase from $500 to $2,000: 15 percent savings ($126).*[5]

Of course, this is an average and can be as high as saving $245 a year in some areas of America. But, if you are like my wife and me, we haven't gotten into an accident in many years. So, by saving $150 a year, we have been able to add that to our retirement fund. I don't want to get too far into the math, but, just to put this in perspective, after ten years of the additional investing, we realized a $3000 increase in our retirement for the risk of having a $1500 higher deductible.

Every situation is unique, so you need to do your own calculations. You could have multiple cars and more expensive vehicles. An average debt-free family can save $1000 per year by analyzing their insurance situation and taking back some risk.

But, if you are not a nerd like I am, all the differences between insurance companies, property values, and interest rates can get a bit confusing. So, it would be worth seeing a financial coach, an advisor, or an insurance agent for a session to save hundreds, or maybe thousands, across all your insurance and savings needs.

This strategy is not just for auto insurance. Use it across your property insurance, life insurance, medical insurance, and beyond. For example, you can adjust the elimination period on your disability insurance to save a few bucks. This move would be a no brainer if you knew you could survive for over six months on your emergency fund without additional Inflow. And, as a bonus, emotionally, the unfortunate situation becomes a worry-free inconvenience!

The critical thing to remember is to have a solid money plan for all the money you are saving. Just because you have a few extra hundred or thousand dollars, now that you are not paying as much in insurance premiums, this doesn't mean it is time to squander it all. You need a plan for your newfound wealth. (HINT: Balance the budget.)

Proper Purpose & Position

What do you value? We get anxious about the wrong things. We are concerned more about our "possessions" than our "purpose."

God has designed

a path to pursue

that leads to the

promise He has

for you.

All our finales are the same. Life beyond this place is our ultimate destination. Are you living for today or tomorrow? I've heard many say, "Live for today, for tomorrow we die"; "Live for the moment. You only live once (YOLO!)"

Like GPS directing you, the driver, to a specific place, you need a forward focus on your life destination. Heaven is home; heaven is the destination. But, when driving your car, even though you know where you are going, you must operate the automobile for the moment, being aware of the traffic, reacting and adjusting the vehicle according to the present circumstances.

You drive according to the moment to arrive safely at the ultimate location. The same applies to your financial decisions. You make daily decisions according to current events for the future destination.

So, what is your purpose? What were you created to create, to do, to change, to provide? God has designed a path to pursue that leads to the promise He has for you. "If you read history, you will find that the Christians who did most for the present world were just those who thought most of the next," Randy Alcorn writes.[6]

Are you doing what God created you to do? This moment in time needs you to be in your place. When working in a position that aligns with your purpose, you realize a joy like no other. But the lack of a plan to get you to the job that you would be most passionate about leads to frustration, worry, and dissatisfaction.

I heard a story of a young couple who grew up together and agreed to go to the same university. They both were there because they loved the colors, the football team, and the school's famous name. They picked the place and a major with little thought and prayer, but they both finished in four years with good grades.

After they graduated and got married, they finally asked God, "What is my purpose? What was I created to do?" They had been feeling a strong call to the mission field, and an opportunity had become available seemingly in perfect timing in their life. School is now complete; no children yet; they were renting and not locked in a lease. They were ready! So they thought.

But there was a significant flaw in their lack of planning up to this point. Now, this couple's grave error was crystal clear. There was no prayer concerning school choice or major or ultimate destination. And now, they had to pay the price for this poor choice. Their combined school loan debt was more than $250,000 and had become a massive roadblock on their path to pursuing their purpose. They found out that the Bible was right: "The borrower is slave to the lender" (Proverbs 33.7 NIV).

Now, for the first time, the young couple prayed and dedicated their lives to the promised purpose God had for them. They repented for leaving Him out of these significant decisions in their lives. Their focus was now on what was still possible.

After working multiple jobs each and living like college kids, they became debt-free by faith and strategy in 26 months. Even though their dream seemed grim, they trusted in the Lord to clear the path. They didn't get depressed and blame others, and they rolled up their sleeves and zeroed in on their target.

We live the best life when we live at this intersection of purpose and position, and God's promise leads us there. "We live our lives today based upon His promised tomorrows" (Pastor Al Toledo, Chicago Tabernacle).

CHAPTER SIX

Be Happy

As we discussed in chapter 5, emergencies can be a real pain in the butt. But they will now only be inconvenient financially. Especially those little pesky emergencies, you know when life is just messing with you. You can just laugh at those now.

Besides covering you when something unexpected occurs, the proper insurance and emergency fund give you a sense of security. Once these tools are in place, you begin to feel good about your plan.

But, before all of this, you sat down with your spouse and accountability partners, drew up a plan, prayed about it, and modified it as the Lord guided you. It gave you a sense of peace, a sense of destiny with your money. It's a huge emotional step in your financial process.

During this process, you realize something spectacular!

Contentment

You realize most of what you used to be worried about is just stuff. Some of it was even junk! You now understand what essentially matters in life.

Jesus says, "Watch out and **guard yourselves from every kind of greed**; because your true life is not made up of the things you own, no matter how rich you may be" (Luke 12:15 GNT).

What are the true riches in life? People save and invest and build up wealth here on earth, but we must keep in mind that true riches will be in heaven. Interestingly, Revelation 21:21 describes heaven as having streets of gold. It is hilarious that the pavement in heaven is the stuff we treasure here on earth.

We are going to look back at this life and laugh. How silly I was in chasing after all those worldly treasures! It's okay to have some stuff, but remember, this life is fleeting. I've never heard of someone on their deathbed saying that all they wish they had ever done is have more stuff. I once heard someone say, "Have you ever seen a hearse pulling a U-Haul?"

See what David wrote in Psalm: "But as for me, **my contentment is not in wealth** but in seeing you and knowing all is well between us. And when I awake in heaven, I will be fully satisfied, for I will see you face-to-face" (Psalm 17:15 TLB).

David was king and had much wealth, for God massively blessed him with worldly possessions. But David's heart, mind, and spirit were focused on what mattered most (also see Psalm 27).

Being happy means being content. But contentment doesn't mean just settling for whatever comes your way, halting your pursuit towards success in a career or entrepreneurship. It just means having the right mindset with money. Give God all the praise for all things and ask for His guidance in all you do and earn.

Paul writes to his son in the faith, Timothy: "But **godliness with contentment is great gain**. For we brought nothing into this world, and it is certain we can carry nothing out. And having food and raiment let us be therewith content" (1 Timothy 6:6-8).

Those verses are followed by a warning to the rich, because God will certainly allow His children to have more than we need. The danger comes when you fall in love with those possessions. As verse 10 states, it's the *love* of money that is the root of all evil. Contentment is the healthy mindset you need to handle abundance. Don't be fearful of your net worth increasing; just prepare yourself to manage great riches properly.

God wants us to be successful and achieve goals and aspirations here in this life, so that we can be a blessing to our families, neighbors, and strangers. If only greedy, selfish people had all the resources, who would feed the hungry and take care of the widow and orphan? That is why we receive according to our ability and willingness to give.

The more you receive, the more you have the responsibility to manage. So, don't ask for more if you are not ready to handle it.

When you read *Divine Provision Meets Generosity Planning*, you will see what a big deal it is. You will see how blessing others and building generational wealth in your family should be a priority. While it is an integral part of your financial plan, it is also the most energizing thing we get to do with God's wealth.

Knowing What You Need

When you budget, you must discuss needs versus wants. This topic is essential to consider with your spouse and your accountability partners. We get confused sometimes and stress out about things and experiences we desire but which don't result in long-term happiness.

By having a plan, you will double-check yourself when a craving for something more arises. For example, when an Amazon ad pops up with something that catches my attention, that feeling comes over me that says, "You need this." I know you have had this sensation, too.

Suddenly, an item we had no intention of buying becomes a priority purchase. Marketers lie to us, saying that this is a once-in-a-lifetime opportunity. "There is only one left," the indicator flashes on the screen. It has turned into an emergency purchase. But then, if you check your plan, you find that this "thing" is not on it.

The beauty of having a plan is that you can add this item or event to the list. Now that you know you want it, you can assess the situation. Will it fit into this month's budget? If not, where can it? How long are you willing to wait? Can something else move if this is more important? The bottom line is, if it is in the plan, you can purchase it with no regrets!

This principle keeps your spending in check. No outsider is restricting you from getting or doing anything. You make the budget; set the boundaries; then pray and let God direct the plan, so these *wants* don't wreck the pursuit of your *needs*.

This strategy will keep you out of debt, from having buyer's remorse, and keep your marriage out of financial hot water. But, most of all, keeping your purchases in check will prevent them from stealing your future joy.

> *God is the highest good of the reasonable creature,*
> *and the enjoyment of him is the only happiness*
> *with which our souls can be satisfied. To go to*

Being prudent

is about choosing

what matters most and

going without the most

worthless things.

*heaven fully to enjoy God, is infinitely better than
the most pleasant accommodations here...Fathers
and mothers, husbands, wives, children, or the
company of earthly friends, are but shadows. But
the enjoyment of God is the substance. These are
but scattered beams, but God is the sun. These are
but streams, but God is the fountain. These are
but drops, but God is the ocean (Jonathan
Edwards).*[1]

Once you've traveled globally and have observed
people's lives around the world, you are either shocked by
what they live without, or you are astonished by what you
can't live without.

I've been to places where a dishwasher would be a
luxury, something an average person would never consider
as a necessity. Air conditioning is for only the upper class
where they live, and a family vehicle is a distant dream.
Their needs include food and basic shelter. But they have
allowed a generational situation to become the norm
instead of allowing God to grow their ability as He
transforms their destiny.

On the other hand, people in a wealthier nation
wouldn't think of having less than a television in each
bedroom, a cell phone and electronic tablet for every child,
and two cars to be upgraded on a regular basis. They need
a bigger house because they have a lot of stuff. But their

perspective could be a little off if their desires don't align with the plan.

Neither situation is necessarily right or wrong. But understanding what God wants you to prioritize is paramount. Knowing what you really need at this time in your life will keep you centered at the intersection. Don't get too far ahead nor too far behind the plan according to your purpose.

Know what really matters and what you really need. "For what is a man advantaged, if he gain the whole world, and lose himself, or be cast away?" (Luke 9:25)

Opportunity Cost

Being prudent is not about not doing what you want to do, what you love to experience, or getting items you desire. It's about choosing what matters most and going without the most worthless things.

You could undoubtedly justify an occasional latte for a special moment. But too many treats will take away from what matters most. It's just an example. Calm down. Don't get mad. This point is not about lattes. This law of opportunity costs can apply to every aspect of life.

Here is the definition of *opportunity cost*: "The fact that when you choose one option, you lose the potential benefits of the other options."[2] For every single purchase, I want you to think to yourself, "What am I giving up?" Don't drive yourself crazy thinking about this, but you need to realize that, if you spend $100 on something in aisle A, you cannot spend that same $100 in aisle B.

For example, I use the opportunity cost principle when explaining why I will never finance a car. Instead of sending money to the bank towards loan repayment, I choose to send that amount to an investment. Once that investment grows to the amount that I can buy the vehicle in cash, I trade that amount of money for the car.

In this example, I take advantage of earning interest as opposed to paying finance charges. But I lose the opportunity to have the car before I could afford it. In the end, I am ahead of where I would have been if I financed it. Therefore, I experience short-term loss for long-term gain.

But even at the point of purchase, I have lost the opportunity to do something else with that same money. Do I want the car or a luxury month-long vacation cruise? Does the car take precedence over donating the cash to my church, knowing that they are building a community center for the neighborhood's grossly underserved children? Or can I do a little of all the above? It's all in praying and planning.

"Be very careful, then, how you live—not as unwise but as wise, making the most of every opportunity, because the days are evil. Therefore do not be foolish, but understand what the Lord's will is" (Ephesians 5:15-17 NIV).

Dr. Anne Bradley writes:

> *The notion of opportunity cost comes from the biblical and economic principle of scarcity. We live in a world of finite time and resources ... Given the reality of scarcity, every choice we make involves forgoing another action or opportunity ... As Christians, we must steward all of our resources with precision and diligence.*[3]

When you don't have a plan, you get blindsided by short-term impulse purchases. Some of these may appear small in amount, but I've seen seemingly insignificant decisions steal one's ultimate dream. Some things need to be denied for other things to be gained.

However, when you know you are working in the sweet spot, that intersection of God's desire for your life and your deepest desires, you find true happiness. You find joy when you can live as you have always dreamed and wake up each morning with no payments on borrowed funds and no regrets because it was all in the plan. There is a sense of calm when you are prepared and in one accord with your spouse in every decision and purchase.

You don't have to worry, and you can certainly be happy when you are operating where prayer meets planning according to the will of God.

Financial Results Using a New Equation

The world is constantly running to the latest new fad in search of happiness. But God has a corner on the market. I always look to the Word to find answers for life, and of course, it never fails. If you want to be daily refreshed, read five Psalms and one Proverb every day.

So, what do these powerful books of the Bible have to say about happiness? The solution should not be any surprise by now. Here is just an appetizer:

"That our garners may be full, affording all manner of store: that our sheep may bring forth thousands and ten thousands in our streets: That our oxen may be strong to labour; that there be no breaking in, nor going out; that there be no complaining in our streets. Happy is that people, that is in such a case: yea, **happy is that people, whose God is the Lord**" (Psalm 144:13-15).

"Put not your trust in princes ... in whom there is no help ... **Happy is he ... whose hope is in the Lord his God**" (Psalm 146:3,5).

"**Happy is the man that findeth wisdom**, and the man that getteth understanding. For the merchandise of it is better than the merchandise of silver, and the gain thereof than fine gold" (Proverbs 3:13-14).

"He that handleth a matter wisely shall find good: and **whoso trusteth in the Lord, happy is he**" (Proverbs 16:20).

When you know

you are working

in the sweet spot,

that intersection of

God's desire

for your life and your

deepest desires,

you find true happiness.

So the secret to happiness is simple. Trust in the Lord your Savior and your God, whom longs to help you in every area of your life. Create a wise plan and stick to it, adjusting it after much prayer, being assured that the plan is the Lord's for your life. You need a strategy, but don't leave out faith. Focus on the infinite riches that God has prepared, living today for the promises of tomorrow.

Here is an equation I bet you've never learned in school:

$$(W \times 0) + P^2 = \infty$$

$(W \times 0)$ = No worry

P^2 = Prayer (pray with thanksgiving $\times$ make your request known)

∞ = Exceeds anything we can understand

So, no worry, plus prayer to the second power (give thanksgiving $\times$ submit your humble requests), equals mind-blowing provision.

I guarantee the results will be more than enough to fulfill your heart's desire and financial needs.

That's powerful! That's true contentment and peace. That's the intersection of faith and strategy.

Part III

Finances by the
Fruit of the Spirit

CHAPTER SEVEN

Your Financial Vital Signs

What is a vital sign anyway? Since I am not a medical professional, and have no desire to become one, the only things I knew about the term "vital sign" was what I leaned from television. Even after going to a routine check-up at the doctor's office, I had no idea what the nurse's job was and why she was doing things that made me feel a bit uncomfortable. All I knew was that her metal objects were cold, having a wooden stick pressing against my tongue was awkward, and the air bag wrapped around my arm was kind of annoying.

So, since I was too embarrassed to ask, I had to do some research, or in my case, an Internet search, to find out what all this was about. I found out from Johns Hopkins website that, "Vital signs are measurements of the body's most basic functions."[1] They prevent misdiagnoses, are useful in detecting or monitoring medical problems and help monitor recovery. The physician can use vital signs to ensure progress towards good health. Well, that is not all that complicated, and now I see why they are so "vital."

Knowing far more about finances than medical science, I immediately saw the similarities between the nurse's routine task of taking a patient's temperature, blood pressure, weight et al., and our need for keeping tabs on our financial wellbeing. This is not only important for our physical health, but is also imperative for our financial fitness. We need to routinely have a checkbook check-up!

There are some medical tests performed during your annual physical that are standard and the same will apply to this financial assessment. Your primary goal is to expose areas of concern so you can address them. Don't be apprehensive. The examination table is not ice cold and the remedies to the most common accounting system ailments are readily available.

But, before I dive into the process of measuring our financial vital signs, I want to make sure we understand why this too is especially important. God is an orderly creator, so we see many parallels in our physical, mental, spiritual, and, yes, financial life. I'm sure you know very well that if you don't catch the signs early, it is easy to get extremely unhealthy in any of these areas. We are naturally driven to do things that worsen these metrics. Bad food, toxic thoughts, worldly influence, and all sorts of temptations are on the prowl aiming to take you down. So be careful as to what drives you.

What Drives You?

I am amazed at how our body works, how it matters what you put into it, and how you take care of it. I struggle with not eating what I know I should not eat and eating the stuff I know I need to eat. And when I yield to the temptations of delicious, saturated fat, gluten, and high fructose corn syrup, I feel fatigued, and those vital signs do not lie.

If I skip cardio, strength training, and stretching, my body gets out of shape quickly. I notice that the more I exercise, the more I enjoy it, but the more I avoid it, the more difficult it is to get started again. We must take care of our bodies, or we will suffer from pain, illness, or suffer the ultimate penalty of premature mortality.

Your mind works in much the same way. Keeping it sharp is essential. You must consume wise and healthy content. If you feed it too much "junk food," like social media and movies, you will feel mental sluggishness. Many sources report that reading, writing, painting, and other brain-stimulating activities keep you feeling motivated in life and even may help prevent brain diseases like dementia and Alzheimer's.

The spirit can also get weak when you abandon God's wisdom. If you don't communicate with God consistently, your spiritual muscles become shriveled. Consuming the truth and resisting worldly noise is essential. Exercise, in this case, includes sharing the Gospel, listening to sermons, praying, and, of course, staying in the Word of God. If you don't, spiritual junk food (i.e. doubt, fear, stress) is readily available to be feasted on.

If we are not careful, we are naturally driven towards things that do us harm. Physical laziness drives us towards quick fixes like fast food, drugs, and every other unwholesome substances. Mental slothfulness leads us to destructive activities like viewing pornography, listening to ungodly music, and getting hooked on video games. Spiritual idleness keeps us searching for counterfeit fulfillment like witchcraft, new age movements and futile religious practices that are unbiblical like praying repetitive prayers.

On the other hand, when we are whole and daily discipline our lives with healthy intentionality, we live the life we were made for. We feel energetic, stable, and locked into the will of God for our lives. It's amazing how attentiveness to your vital signs can drastically transform your life's path.

What about money? Staying on top of your budget, goals, and mission is imperative. When I become lazy with finances, spending carelessly, and outside my plan, I've noticed that the dollars and cents wander away. There is no wonder that terms like liquid and currency refer to the use of money.

We all need to stay healthy, not just physically, mentally, and spiritually, but financially as well. Have you ever looked into your money mirror (personal accounting system) and noticed that you were getting a bit financially flabby? It is time to build that money muscle. Even if the flabbiness is not apparent, you may have deeper health issues within your stewardship. So, let's talk about financial vital signs.

In a moment, we will look at your financial heart and make sure it is pumping Inflow and Outgo as it should. We will explore the hands and feet of your accounting, inspecting your actions. Finally, we'll check your head to find out how your money mindset is ticking.

But first, I want to debunk the horrible lie that money is immoral on its own. Nor is it good. These are myths. I hear people refer to money as "filthy lucre," but though cash may be unsanitary materially, it has no desire to do good or bad. Money has no choice.

The manager of it has all the say. It's the **love of money** that's the root of all evil (1 Timothy 6:10), not the money itself. And as you will see in the next chapter, when you use money with love, you end up with joy. When is the

When you keep

your financial health

in check,

your savings account

balance becomes

available to do

wonderful things.

last time you heard someone use money and joy in the same sentence?

If greed or envy consumes you, or you accumulate wealth through theft or deception, your net worth will be cancerous to the core. But if you want to help other people, bless your family, and manage God's wealth with His wisdom, you have the right approach.

In order to help others, your financial situation must be healthy. Like no one has a perfect physique, it is impossible to be in a position where you can't improve your financial health. You will discover areas of weakness by checking your vital signs.

When you keep your financial health in check, your savings account balance becomes available to do wonderful things. But a malignant money mindset will do you, as well as everyone around you, harm.

Checking Your Pulse

Be honest with yourself. Do you ever have desires to do things with money that you know are not right? Now that you are a child of God, you can ask the Holy Spirit to reveal every area that needs improvement. Ask the Great Physician to check your pulse.

Jesus said: "If therefore ye have not been faithful in the unrighteous mammon, who will commit to your trust the true riches? And if ye have not been faithful in that which is another man's, who shall give you that which is your own? No servant can serve two masters: for either he will hate the one, and love the other; or else he will hold to the one, and despise the other. **Ye cannot serve God and mammon**" (Luke 16:11-13).

The term "mammon" in this context is a word we don't use today. So let's dig into the definition. The Encyclopedia Britannica says that mammon is a "biblical term for riches, often used to describe the debasing influence of material wealth. The term was used by Jesus in His famous Sermon on the Mount and also appears in The Gospel According to Luke. Medieval writers commonly interpreted it as an evil demon or god. Since the 16th century, mammon has been used to negatively describe the pursuit of wealth and has been used in both religious and secular contexts."[2]

So, mammon represents the evil use of money. When you have a tendency towards cheating on your taxes, stealing from others, or idolizing things, the spirit of mammon is present. The cure is turning to Jesus.

I think of mammon as financial heart disease. If there is not enough blood circulation throughout the body, you can tell by measuring your pulse. You can lose feeling in your hands and feet. Also, your brain needs adequate blood flow.

A weak pulse, a rapid pulse, or an erratic pulse are all not in the expected range. Cholesterol-clogged coronary arteries are many times revealed by a high pulse-rate.

Similarly, mammon clogs your financial arteries and may lead to your financial heart eventually failing.

Low blood pressure or a blockage can also result in a weak pulse. Mammon blocks the blood of Jesus from doing its job. The blood of Jesus has the power to deliver, so the blood is not the problem. But when you let mammon block it, you allow worldly desires to snuff out the entrance of the truth.

Your entire financial body depends on this critical vital sign. Every time you go into the doctor's office for a checkup, one of the nurse's first duties is to check your pulse. As you will read in the last three chapters, your financial heart, hands + feet, and head, all need adequate and proper blood flow. So, don't ignore the potential symptoms.

The Bible puts it so succinctly: "Remember Lot's wife" (Luke 17:32). In other words, check your pulse. Worldly possessions and a lifestyle laced with mammon consumed Lot's wife. She died because she looked back, longing to return to the pleasures of that life, instead of focusing forward on the path God was directing their family. Check your pulse by recognizing when you are being affected by the mesmerizing lure of the material world.

These issues can sneak up on you because many times everything seems to be in working order. You can seem perfectly healthy on the outside when there is plaque building up in your veins on the inside. Your savings account looks good; your budget looks good; you are sharing wealth regularly. All the while, a hint of pride grows because your pulse has gone unchecked. By the time you notice an issue, it is no longer insignificant but begins choking your financial health.

The essential elements of God's remedy are: salvation, dependence on prayer, and daily reading of the Bible. It is important to reiterate these essentials of relationship because, when things are going well, we can forget. I've also mentioned the guidance by the Holy Spirit; but next you will see how to keep your financial health in tip-top condition by applying the Fruit of the Spirit to your financial strategy.

But before we go there, let's check your temperature.

Taking Your Temperature

I notice that when the nurse or doctor takes my temperature, it must fall within a small range. The ideal temp is 98.6°F (37°C), a very specific target. That's how you need to assess your financial temperature, better known as financial integrity.

"Better is the poor that **walketh in his uprightness**, than he that is perverse in his ways, though he be rich" (Proverbs 28:6). You should make no room for lack of integrity. I like how the word *uprightness* implies posture. If you are dishonest or crooked in your dealing with money, your financial life is hunched over and disformed.

Using the archery analogy, you can have your crosshairs perfectly aligned on your target, but if your arrow has no integrity (meaning it is bent out of shape), you will miss your target. Take a minute and think about that. It is possible to have knowledge of God's wisdom for the wealth He has given you to manage, and yet abuse it.

If fact, this is the situation that Judas Iscariot, one of Jesus's disciples, was in. He was in the presence of All Mighty God, listening to His instructions directly from His mouth, but he allowed corruption into his heart. The book of John presents the fact that he was stealing money from the treasury instead of giving to the poor. It went so far as to infect his entire being, eventually leading to his death.

Just like your body temperature, this vital sign must be monitored regularly and taken extremely seriously. Infinium Medical states: "Irregular body temperature is an early sign of an infection. Even if you feel fine, ensure you are maintaining a healthy body temperature by checking your vitals. Abnormal fluctuations in body temperature are cause for concern."[3]

When there is an indication of a financial ailment in your life, you know you have an infectious disease that you must attend to immediately. 1 Corinthians 6:10 lists some of these viruses: theft, greed, cheating, and extortion. There are many more including jealousy and envy. All of these infections attack an otherwise healthy financial strategy.

And just like a high temp, there are early warning signs. Infinium Medical goes on: "Sweating, clamminess, and other disruptions to your body temperature are early signs that your body is fighting off a virus. Monitoring body temperature allows you to take preventive measures to detect problems and prevent spreading an illness to others."

If you get sweaty or clammy when doing something wrong, that's a good sign. That means your conscience is still intact and you are listening to the Holy Spirit, like I mentioned in Chapter 2.

Once you begin being dishonorable with money and have no physical alerts, you are getting into dangerous territory. You may have financial heat stroke or monetary anhidrosis, a condition where you don't perspire when you should. These viruses are not to be ignored.

And, yes, materialism, covetousness, and all other financial germs are contagious. Therefore, you should also choose your close friends wisely. Don't forget the principles in Chapter 3; now you can see why they are significant. When you have trustworthy brothers and sisters around you, they may observe you have a fever before you do.

When someone becomes numb to their financial failures, it may be because of past hurt and pain, a traumatic event, or influence from one's upbringing. No matter the cause, the antidote is the same.

If you struggle with a monetary infection, never fear, the cure is near. Turning towards Jesus and away from the darkness will always make you well again. That nasty list of transgressions in 1 Corinthians 6 is followed by the cure: "And such were some of you: but ye are washed, but ye are sanctified, but ye are justified in the name of the Lord Jesus, and by the Spirit of our God" (1 Corinthians 6:11).

If you have not been washed clean and cured by the blood of Jesus, I implore you to turn back to Chapter 1 and accept Him as Lord of your life. You will be made whole, and the result will be a clean bill of health spiritually and financially.

Your Financial Heart, Hands + Feet, and Head

Now that we have checked your pulse and made sure your temperature is in the ideal range, it is time to check your heart, hands + feet, and head. The best way I have found to gauge and improve the health of these critical financial body parts is to consume the Holy Spirit's "super fruit." This is known as the Fruit of the Spirit.

I call them super fruit because the health industry has promoted certain fruit as super fruit since they dramatically improve your physical health. For example, strawberries and blueberries can lower blood pressure and protect blood vessels. In the same way, these spiritual fruit will help keep your vital signs in the best range. While grapefruit, kiwi, and apples may help you lose weight, the Fruit of the Spirit are going to help you lose that financial flab.

Have you ever heard someone say, "I'm not good at eating healthy"? Well, that is a strange statement. Are they ready "bad" at consuming food that will improve their memory, weight, vitality, and overall life? Probably not. What they really mean is that they love unhealthy food so much that they are not willing to trade some of it for food that tastes differently. It may be artificial sugar, or saturated fat, or one of the many other tasty alternatives that have stolen their taste buds away from naturally healthy super fruit.

I've always found it incredible to think how I can eat so much nutrition-less food that something good for me can taste unpleasant. But the good news is that, if you work in those healthy foods into your diet, you cultivate a taste for them and even desire them. That happened to me with bananas, believe it or not. I think I ate one too many Pop Tarts in my twenties. I blamed my disdain for bananas on the texture. Then I even had a minor allergic reaction to them. But I stopped all the sugary packaged pastries and started eating fruit for breakfast little by little. Over a short period, I grew to love bananas and the allergic reactions disappeared. Now I've lost my desire for Pop Tarts, and I'm healthier for it.

The same thing happens with the Fruit of the Spirit. Just like healthy food, once you make it a part of your daily life, you will feel the positive effects. You may just forget about the sweet but dangerous counterfeits you used to enjoy. So, be warned; you may not like the taste the first time you try them, but give the Holy Spirit freedom to fill you with these nine nutrients.

In the last three chapters, I would like to present an application of the Fruit of the Spirit to your finances. These nine attributes describe how you can live in one accord with the Holy Spirit. If God is living in you and through you, His guidance should include the money He has placed in your possession.

If you want to be whole and wholesome, you want to live by the Fruit of the Spirit. This assessment is an excellent measuring stick or gauge of your present and future success with money.

Paul's letter to the Galatians includes the Fruit of the Spirit: "But the Holy Spirit produces this kind of fruit in our lives: **love, joy, peace, patience, kindness, goodness, faithfulness, gentleness, and self-control**. There is no law against these things! Since we are living by the Spirit, let us follow the Spirit's leading in every part of our lives" (Galatians 5:22-23,25 NLT).

He didn't write "some parts of our lives," but "every part of our lives." That includes finances.

I find it interesting that this chapter ends with: "Let us not become conceited, or provoke one another, or be jealous of one another" (Galatians 5:26 NLT).

If God is living in you and through you,

His guidance should include the money

He has placed in your possession.

So, these improper views of wealth were just as common then as they are today. Vanity is so prevalent today that we have a magazine by that name. We even have television shows admitting our idolizing of other people's talents and wealth. Envy is alive and well. And, provoking one another to make more money, spend more, and have more saturates every advertisement.

However, as Christians, we are not of this world. Heaven is our eventual home. But while here on earth, we need guidance by the Spirit to manage God's wealth well.

I will divide the nine Fruit of the Spirit into three parts: your financial heart, your financial hands + feet, and your financial head. Just like your body, you need these to work in harmony together and not war against one another. Also, you need them all to be in full operation, not just one or two.

Your financial heart will include having love, joy, and peace with money. The hands and feet of your financial plan include working through patience (long-suffering), kindness, and goodness. As for your head, or money mindset, you must win the struggle when it comes to faithfulness, gentleness (meekness), and self-control (temperance).

Download the companion poster from the INTERSECTION Resource Page, and let's explore where the fruit of the Spirit and your financial plan intersect.

intersection.zeroinfinancial.com[4]

CHAPTER EIGHT

Your Financial Heart

The heart is one of your most essential organs. The debate comes down to either the brain or the heart as to which has greater significance. Both are extraordinary. The heart feeds the vital life substance, blood, to all parts of the body. And no part, not even the brain, can survive for long without blood.

Very Well Health reports:

> *A person becomes unconscious quickly during cardiac arrest. This usually happens within 20 seconds after the heart stops beating. Without the oxygen and sugars it needs to function, the brain is*

> *unable to deliver the electrical signals needed to maintain breathing and organ function...When cardiac arrest occurs, cardiopulmonary resuscitation (CPR) must be started within two minutes. After three minutes, global cerebral ischemia—the lack of blood flow to the entire brain—can lead to brain injury that gets progressively worse. By nine minutes, severe and permanent brain damage is likely. After 10 minutes, the chances of survival are low.*[1]

We will look at the amazing brain in chapter ten, but for now let's explore the heart of the matter. The human heart has been described as your body's engine. Likewise, your financial heart is the engine that keeps your entire financial plan running. As we saw in chapter seven, by checking our pulse, irregularities with the heart indicate financial health issues. So, treating your heart with special care would be wise.

"Guard your heart above all else, for it determines the course of your life" (Proverbs 4:23 NLT). Once the heart stops beating, there is little time before severe damage is done. I can't believe that it only takes ten minutes after cardiac arrest before the chances of survival are considered dismal. I know in my life I have taken heart health for granted. But if one waits too long, it can be too late.

Many people think nothing of their financial heart's health and ignore the warning signs. I always say that as long as you are breathing it is never too late to get financially fit, but the later you wait, the more difficult it will be.

Thank goodness your financial heart's warning signs can be loud and clear—if you know what to listen for. Early signs are always important for avoiding major injury. You do not want to get to the point of having a financial heart attack. So pay close attention to how and what you are feeding your heart as we walk through these first three fruit.

Love

What has love got to do with finances? A lot! If you follow the path blazed by your banking statements, you will soon find what you love. Jesus taught in Matthew 6:21, "For where your treasure is, there will your heart be also." Your heart and things you value most are tightly linked.

Do you love experiences or items? Check your bank statement: it will tell you.

Do you love yourself more than others? Compare last year's generosity to the amount you spent on self indulgences.

How does your investment in business, retirement, and legacy compared to your investing in missions, charity, and the local church?

Through your financial heart flows currency towards the things you love most.

These are all questions, not to convict you, but to provoke thought around understanding where your heart is. Through your financial heart flows currency towards the things you love most. If you live for God's purpose for your life, you will use His resources to fulfill that purpose, and you will be passionate about it.

Passion also comes from the heart. I've always noticed that the more I am working within my purpose, the more passionate I am. And the more passionate I get, the more generous I am with the compensation I've received from the work. I just want to give and see others blessed when my heart is right. God is a giver; and the spirit of giving is from Him. If you genuinely desire to understand this characteristic of God—and you should—read *Divine Provision Meets Generosity Planning* where I explore it deeply.

When we love selflessly, we give from our resources and help others who can't help themselves. To do the opposite would be a sign of a heart condition.

Your resources include more than monetary resources, and sometimes only showing love in a purely financial way can be very unloving. For example, constantly bailing someone out because of your love for them without ever showing them how to earn money for themselves is unloving and unhelpful.

Other financial heart ailments include theft and covetousness. God gave the Ten Commandments in Exodus 20, including "Thou shalt not steal" and "Thou shalt not covet." Taking without permission or legal right is not loving. And to yearn for someone else's possessions, which is covetousness, shows your need for a heart checkup.

But in the new covenant, Jesus takes this to a whole new level: "But I say unto you which hear, **Love your enemies,** do good to them which hate you, Bless them that curse you, and pray for them which despitefully use you. **Give to every man that asketh of thee**; and of him that taketh away thy goods ask them not again" (Luke 6:27-28,30).

Our Lord and Savior, who gave His life for us when we despised Him, knows a lot about giving to those who don't "deserve" it. He not only demonstrated true love, but commands us to follow His example.

In this same passage of scripture, He tells us that these acts of love don't go unnoticed by our Heavenly Father; there is a reward waiting for you: "But love ye your enemies, and do good, and lend, hoping for nothing again; **and your reward shall be great,** and ye shall be the children of the Highest: for he is kind unto the unthankful and to the evil" (Luke 6:35).

For nearly ten years, I was in the US Navy, and for six of those years, I served aboard the USS Milius (DDG-69) which is a Guided Missile Destroyer. When I arrived at the ship, I learned that the command's motto was "Alii Prae Me," which is Latin for "Others Before Myself."[2]

That seemed unusual to me. I was expecting a ship with such heavy armament to have a slogan projecting bold and intimidating words, threatening all who dare to approach. As the website We Are the Mighty presents, here are just a few of what they list as the "Coolest Military Unit Mottos":

- "Whatever It Takes"—USA, 1st Battalion, 4th Marines
- "Molon Labe" (Greek for "Come and take them")—Greece, Army unit
- "Better to die than to be a coward"— UK, The Royal Gurkha Rifles, British Army
- "Lerne leiden ohne zu klagen!" (German for "learn to suffer without complaining!")—Germany, Kampfschwimmer, Navy unit[3]

The words on my warship's crest were not like these. My unit's slogan was unique, and unusually loving, so I had to learn the reason behind this rarity.

The ship's namesake was Captain Paul L. Milius, a POW/MIA from the Vietnam War. He sacrificed his life for his aircrew during combat action over Laos in 1968. Thinking of others first was his natural reaction.

After his plane was hit by an explosive and could not be saved, Captain Milius took the controls from the pilot so that all crew members could bail out to safety. "Of the eight surviving crew members of the initial blast, all but Captain Milius were safely rescued on the ground."

I would imagine he could have bailed out first. He didn't have to take the controls and steady the plane for his fellow crew. But, he knew his duty and responsibility to serve others first. He followed his heart.

So, being assigned to a ship named after such a magnificent hero was a great honor for me. I knew I wanted to lead my life in much the same way.

Remember, at the end of Chapter 3, the verse I recommended meditating on: "Greater love hath no man than this, that a man lay down his life for his friends" (John 15:13).

Operating your financial plan with the mission of thinking of others' needs first is true love. You may not die for someone as Captain Milius did for his crew, and Jesus did for all of us, but you should always show love. It may cost you truly little or may require that you sacrifice deeply at times. Don't do it only for the generous reward you will receive in heaven. Do it for the sake of loving others before yourself.

Joy

My wife and I have been blessed in more ways than we could ever document. And I give God all the glory that we have continued to place decisions in the right priority. Genuine joy has been the result.

The best priority is to use the simple acrostic J-O-Y: Jesus first, Others second, Yourself last. This order keeps your spending in check, governs your giving every year, and prioritizes your savings goals.

Don't fall for the "pay yourself first" trap. This saying came about because people do not save enough money in their retirement account, ending up penniless in their later years. This not so grand finale results from not having a plan, or having a plan without a foundation of prayer and generosity.

A balanced plan yields genuine joy. When Jesus is at the center of your life and financial decisions, you have the perfect start. The next step, mentioned in the previous section, includes love for others as part of the plan. You can then realize joy because you did these two steps first.

The Apostle Paul mentions in the chapter listing the Fruit of the Spirit: "For all the law is fulfilled in one word, even in this; Thou shalt **love thy neighbour as thyself**" (Galatians 5:14). This means you should treat other people at least as well as you treat yourself.

I don't want to go further without saying, never feel bad because you cannot provide as much as you wish you could. Giving should be a part of the short-term and long-term plan. As I mentioned, generosity is a topic I expound on in *Divine Provision Meets Generosity Planning*, but I have also written several blog posts on the subject if you need more direction in this area. Read them here: zeroinfinancial.com/generouslygive[4]

Only God can produce authentic joy. So, you need to tap the source to allow it to flow through your life. Let's turn to the book of Luke to review the Christmas story.

Jesus is born, and Joseph and Mary are wrapping Him up in a blanket and laying Him in the manger. Then suddenly, an angel appears. "And the angel said unto them, 'Fear not: for, behold, **I bring you good tidings of great joy**, which shall be to all people. For unto you is born this day in the city of David a Saviour, which is Christ the Lord'" (Luke 2:10-11).

The birth of our Savior was "Great Joy!" You must have Christ at the center of your money plan for great joy to fill your financial heart. Do you see why I had to start this book with the message: "You must be born again?" It's the only way to experience real joy! And indeed, by committing your life to Jesus Christ, you gave yourself the greatest gift ever.

You may be thinking, Jesus first, others second, what about me? Don't worry; there will be plenty left over for you. It is not wrong to treat yourself, enjoy your wealth, and live a prosperous life. The problem is when you have the priority backward: YOJ. It is an unexplainable financial law; just ask anyone who has a strong financial plan. Every person I've met who regularly blesses others is really, really blessed. And far too often, people who are struggling financially have put themselves first.

As I said in Chapter 2, love and obedience are bound together. Likewise, joy and love are attached at the hip.

When Jesus taught how your life could be full of joy, He said, "If ye keep my commandments, ye shall abide in my love; even as I have kept my Father's commandments, and abide in his love. **These things have I spoken unto you, that my joy might remain in you, and that your joy might be full**" (John 15:10-11).

Do you want the heart of your financial plan to be full of pleasure and joy? Keep the Word of God in your heart. I love the way David ends Psalm 16, for we should pray this way every day. "Thou wilt shew me the path of life: in **thy presence is fulness of joy**; at thy right hand there are pleasures for evermore" (Psalm 16:11).

Pleasure is the most desired outcome when using money. I have found that no one really wants money. When asked about one's deepest desires of the heart, I get responses that range from leisure to necessities to generosity. But in all the answers, I saw that the things or the experience desired brought some pleasure. The money was only a tool in pursuit of the product.

This joy is not fleeting like the world promotes. I love a good amusement park as much as anyone, but its pleasures are not lasting. As the psalmist exclaims, the fullness of joy is found in the Lord's presence. God possesses endless pleasures, and they are in His hand because He is always ready to give them to you and me. If you bring your heart's desire to Him, He will fulfill them—guaranteed.

I love the Christmas season because it is the time of year when everyone is exposed to the word "joy" more than any other time of year. There are songs playing in the stores with a joyous melody, and the word is sung throughout. Decorations everywhere have "joy" in lights and vibrant colors. Even if the patrons do not know why the word is being used during this holiday, they understand it is a season of giving.

Understanding that God's gift of His one and only Son was a moment of Great Joy, you can now see why we get such joy out of giving to others. God put that desire within our hearts. You can tell that your financial heart is in great shape when you get abundant joy from being a blessing to others. And when you do, you will be blessed too, for you will be many other people's "other."

Peace

It is just as essential for your financial heart to be at peace as it is to be full of love and joy. We live in a time where anxiety is skyrocketing; worry has permeated every neighborhood, and financial stress is an everyday occurrence. The pharmaceutics industry is booming because of the demand for drugs that calm the nerves or allay depression. None of them offer peace. But this does not have to be your destiny.

Let me assure you that a life without worry is the better life. God wants you to have peace.

Many of us think that peace is nearly impossible, but I want to challenge your definition of it. Do you envision peace as not having any lack? Would you describe peace as a life without conflict? Is your understanding of peace not having to go to work? Be honest with yourself and write down your personal definition of peace, then come back and continue reading.

If you don't know what peace looks like, let me give you a definition. True peace is enjoying rest in the knowledge that God is in control. But, let me go one step further. To know that God is in control, you need to believe in God.

It all starts with knowing who God is and understanding who you are, and the relationship you have with Him. When you acknowledge God as Creator, Father, Provider, Savior, Protector, you will find peace. When you understand God is omnipotent, omniscient, omnipresent, and He lives in you, loves through you, and for you, you realize peace.

Go back to your personal definition and pray that God would take all of your preconceived thoughts of peace, and breathe new life into them. Allow Him to go far beyond the limits you have placed on this area in your life. These words are so comforting. "And the peace of God, which passeth all understanding, **shall keep your hearts and minds** through Christ Jesus" (Philippians 4:7). God goes far beyond those little needs we bring to Him.

Financial success is

not only realized when

you have possessions

or money but when you

have peace concerning

your ability to manage

it for its rightful owner,

God.

God provides for all your needs, and He guards you, protecting you from harm so you may enjoy those provisions. He guards your financial heart. The best insurance policy you will ever have is salvation through Jesus Christ, and this policy doesn't cost you a penny!

Notice this verse says, "your hearts and minds." Your financial heart and head are tightly integrated and influence each other, so expect some overlap here. Science confirms this connection: "Traditionally, the study of communication pathways between the head and heart has been approached from a rather one-sided perspective...We have learned, however, that communication between the heart and brain actually is a dynamic, ongoing, two-way dialogue, with each organ continuously influencing the other's function."[5]

This book is about managing not only wealth but your thoughts about wealth. Financial success is not only realized when you have possessions or money but when you have peace concerning your ability to manage it for its rightful owner, God.

If your thoughts and heart are not right, you will be a miserable manager. Have you ever met someone with many possessions but didn't have peace? That is because they have money, but they haven't found this secret to financial success. Yes, they have riches, but it comes with unrelenting stress.

When I begin a coaching relationship with an individual or family, they inevitably are worried that they cannot stick to their budget. They have doubt and are very concerned about their discipline and capability. As far as budgeting is concerned, there is no peace in their heart.

One month into the program, there is a shift in their outlook, and they begin to realize financial peace, sometimes for the first time in their lives. No, they didn't win the lottery or have a rich uncle die. They simply stopped trying to do all the work themselves and allowed God to enter their mess. Their financial situation hadn't drastically changed, but their financial heart has been transformed.

Watch out for the fake peace the world teaches, which looks a lot like compromise. "Thus says the LORD concerning the prophets who **lead my people astray, who cry 'Peace' when they have something to eat**, but declare war against him who puts nothing into their mouths" (Micah 3:5 ESV). In this passage of scripture, God is angry with the leaders who tied peace with their own selfish gain.

God's peace doesn't circumvent or disregard reality, but instead keeps you grounded during your circumstance. "'For the mountains may depart and the hills be removed, but **my steadfast love shall not depart from you, and my covenant of peace shall not be removed**,' says the LORD, who has compassion on you" (Isaiah 54:10 ESV). Even when you may not be in the best financial situation, you can have peace. Instead of being subject to prosperous times as in the world's peace, God's peace is ever present through all times and ultimately results in true wealth.

So, if you desire to have peace in your heart, you must get in control of your money mindset. Your thoughts will control whether you have peace. The following verses give you the prescription to follow if you want to access it: "Whatsoever things are true, whatsoever things are honest, whatsoever things are just, whatsoever things are pure, whatsoever things are lovely, whatsoever things are of good report; if there be any virtue, and if there be any praise, **think on these things**. Those things, which ye have both learned, and received, and heard, and seen in me, do: **and the God of peace shall be with you**" (Philippians 4:8b-9).

Determine what you need to work on by taking an honest look at your fiscal EKG, measuring the love, joy, and peace signals flowing to and from the financial heart. Allow God to heal your heart, and I promise you will see positive results very quickly. "The Lord looks down from heaven and sees the whole human race. From his throne, he observes all who live on the earth. **He made their hearts**, so he understands everything they do" (Psalm 33:13-15 NLT).

CHAPTER NINE

Your Financial Hands and Feet

Looking at the heart first is imperative because the heart provides life-giving blood to the rest of your physical body. The same holds true financially speaking. Your financial heart pumps love, joy and peace into the otherwise dormant digits recorded in a bank account. Also, just like blood feeds your literal hands and feet, your financial extremities operate best when the heart is healthy and fully functional.

Medical News Today points out that when the heart is not able to do its job, there may be wide range of symptoms, many of which appear in the hand and feet.

"One of the most common symptoms of poor circulation is numbness and tingling in the hands and feet." Another problem listed is that "reduced blood flow causes the hands and feet to feel much colder than the rest of the body." Yet another result is that "poor circulation affects the body's ability to heal, which can lead to ulcers in the legs and feet." The article states, "These symptoms can affect a person's quality of life and may even cause severe complications."[1]

There is no wonder that the next three fruit of the Spirit have trouble functioning in one's finances when the first three are weak. Just like your actual hands and feet are the means for getting work done, enjoying leisure activities, and pursuing life's tasks and goals, these fruit help you fulfill the purpose for which you use money.

Thank God He gives us symptoms like numbness and tingling, so we can correct an issue before it becomes terminal! If you notice that your monetary hands and feet have become cold, you can look back at the heart of the issue.

Could this be a sign that patience, kindness, and goodness are not directing your financial activities? Don't wait until there is too much damage to heal. These next three fruit of the Spirit are far too important.

This is where love is put into action as it is said: "It's time to walk the walk." Ministries that spread the Gospel of Jesus Christ can not operate without financial support from those who kindly give. And as children of God, we all should be obedient to the Great Commission. It takes money, time, hospitality, and many other resources which God provides to us to do this great work.

It takes those who preach but also those that support and dedicate their lives to work behind the scenes to bring the message of salvation to all corners of the earth. It all belongs in your plan and is put into motion via financial hand and feet. "How beautiful are the feet of those who bring good news!" (Romans 10:15b NIV)

Patience (Longsuffering)

I must admit that patience is one of the two fruit of the Spirit that I struggle with the most. What about you? (I'll let you guess what the second one is.) It's a good thing God spread them out, one in the middle of the list and the other at the end.

Patience can be unbelievably difficult, but it is always rewarding. Times of waiting yield powerful results, mainly because they create an atmosphere for the Spirit to speak to you and for you to think before you act. Your hands and feet want to go, if you are like me, and getting things done energizes you. But let's not be too hasty.

In Chapter 4, I mentioned Philippians 4:6 in its reference to proper prayer. But modern translations use the phrase "Do not worry" as opposed to the old English version, which says, "Do not be anxious." Anxiety is the opposite of being patient: The Lord hears your requests and will provide in His timing, which is always perfect. Yes, pray and wait on the Lord.

A few years ago, my wife brought home some seeds she received as a gift. They were in an unmarked little Ziploc bag, and we did not know what type of plant they would bear. We didn't plant them and ended up forgetting about them. A couple years later we found the bag in a drawer while Spring cleaning. They looked just like they had been when she brought them home, so we put them in some soil to see what would happen.

I watered it, prayed over it, and checked on it day after day. Then one day there was a small green stem breaking forth from the dirt. I'm not a gardener, so it blows me away that this little seed that had been sitting dormant for years could produce life. God is such an amazing Creator. A little faith, nurturing, the right conditions, and patience will bring forth growth.

Then I understood how prayer over someone's dormant financial situation could bring forth life and prosperity, though not instantly.

In fact, we see this prayer-patience relationship all over scripture. This intersection is one of the more prevalent, for sure. When you need help in any financial situation, this is where you want to aim.

If you are looking at a financial mess you've gotten yourself into with money, your immediate solution should be, **"Rejoicing in hope; patient in tribulation; continuing instant in prayer"** (Romans 12:12).

When you are asking God for an outpouring of aid in a friend or family member's time of need, remember what the psalmist said: "**I waited patiently for the Lord**; and he inclined unto me, and heard my cry" (Psalm 40:1).

And if you can't see any way out of a bad financial situation: "But if we hope for that we see not, then do we **with patience wait for it**" (Romans 8:25).

But you are tired, and you are ready to give up: "The Lord himself will fight for you. **Just stay calm**" (Exodus 14:14 NLT).

Even when you are doing the right thing, and someone else is making far more money than you, doing things unethically: "**Rest in the Lord, and wait patiently for him**: fret not thyself because of him who prospereth in his way, because of the man who bringeth wicked devices to pass" (Psalm 37:7).

Patience plus prayer produces perfect prosperity. Whatever you put your hands to and wherever your feet lead you, do it intentionally. This is by far the best way.

Your financial hands and feet go the way of your heart and head. If you don't have the first three fruit of the Spirit working together, it is tempting to get impatient and work without questioning immoral activity. Remember that lack of blood circulation bringing about tingling? Don't ignore the symptoms. And, as we will see with the last three fruit of the Spirit, without those being in place, you could be impatient and resort to unethical practices to get ahead.

Patience

plus prayer

produces

perfect prosperity.

There is no amount of wealth worth getting impatient for because God gives you the perfect portion, and He is always on time. But when you get ahead of the will of God, wealth becomes a curse instead of a blessing.

I remember one of the biggest financial boo-boos we ever made was because of our lack of patience: buying a Florida timeshare while on a Hawaii vacation. Marketers of timeshares use tactics to pressure you into deciding without having time to think about your purchase. It is not illegal but seems to be borderline unethical. Either way, their marketing method seems to work well, or they would not be in business.

Well, the next thing I know, I had convinced myself and my wife that this would be a good buy; but of course, we did not consult the Lord. That thing ended up being like leprosy to our financial hands and feet. Looking back at that Medical News Today article, now I know we had developed an ulcer in our financial feet, and it made it very difficult for us to walk in our purpose. After six long years, God delivered us from this horrible mistake.

We learned a valuable lesson, and now I have advised others how to avoid this blunder. One of the best ways to help yourself is to buy nothing over a certain amount of money without praying about it and sleeping on it. If you know and agree to this rule in advance, this habit will keep you and your family from jumping ahead in these situations.

Pray always for all things. And leave the decision for tomorrow. You will wake up with more clarity and avoid huge financial errors.

This not only includes spending but also applies to giving. God may not want you to give to a specific charity or a fund-raising event. Not that there may be anything wrong with the cause; it just may not be the financial target you should aim at right now. A rash decision today could create a conflict for something you never knew to be ready for tomorrow.

Kindness

Where love is coming from your financial heart, kindness stems from your hands and feet. Now that you are a Christian, you must walk the walk. We have covered the mindset of money; now, it's time to put those thoughts into action. "Do unto others" just got real!

You may see people in financial despair as you have never seen before. But something happens when you use God's wealth with His wisdom. Your eyes are more aware of the devil's schemes. You will see an opportunity to help, advise, and guide others out of their financial predicaments.

But when you do, always be kind. Remember where you came from and how horrible you felt about squandering God's resources. Be considerate with every answer as you give counsel to fellow brothers and sisters. Kindness is love in action.

I believe a big part of kindness is forgiveness. If you ever want to be kind and feel the results most powerfully, write a letter to someone who owes you money, stating that they are forgiven and owe you no more. Stamp the letter with big red letters: PAID IN FULL.

For sure, one of the kindest moments you can be a part of is forgiving debts. Isn't this what God did for you? "And **be ye kind one to another**, tenderhearted, forgiving one another, even as God for Christ's sake hath forgiven you" (Ephesians 4:32).

The most extraordinary kindness is when the recipient doesn't deserve it. If you are waiting to do something kind to someone when they deserve compassion, you will wait a long time. People rarely deserve the kindness received, especially forgiveness. We still don't deserve God's forgiveness, but He withholds none.

And again, please, don't believe that everyone you are kind to, financially, verbally, or emotionally, will receive it with gratitude. You may not even get a thank you. But that is not the reason to use your monetary or non-monetary hands and feet to exercise kindness to all. Be kind with no expectation of reciprocal action.

There are situations that involve money management which are very difficult for people to maintain a Godly mindset. These situations involve others questioning or even demanding that you give, save, or spend the way they see you should as opposed to your own convictions. People can easily overstep the necessary boundaries of relationship and put unnecessary pressure on you to give. This could relate to a friendship, a relative, or even an online ministry you occasionally sow into. Then you can easily become bitter and unkind because of their remarks. Don't fall for this trap. You should be kind in every situation, even to those who criticize your financial strategy and think they know better.

Also, there will be situations where you disagree with other's decisions. Sometimes it would be a good idea for you to counsel them. But, many times, it is kinder to bite your tongue and pray for them in your private time. You are not the Holy Spirit. Allow Him to work and know that the Master is in control. It is not your job to determine the best use of someone else's resources, and any flippant comments will not be kind or helpful.

This common occurrence reminds me of a parable Jesus told where the lord of the vineyard contracted to pay every laborer the same amount, no matter how long they worked. The workers who were there all day complained about the amount of money those that were hired in the last hour received. The lord responded to them: "Friend, I do thee no wrong: **didst not thou agree with me for a penny**? Take that thine is, and go thy way: I will give unto this last, even as unto thee. Is it not lawful for me to do what I will with mine own? Is thine eye evil, because I am good?" (Matthew 20:13-15)

This is a warning to those who take issue with someone else's financial decisions. Don't be unkind; be good. Be kind by not inserting yourself as the manager of someone else's plan. Know that you don't see the complete picture, and if you trust God, who sees and knows everything, your hands and feet will not enter into evil.

Remember that the truth always flies on two wings, meaning we must look at the other side of the story. Sometimes it may not be beneficial to give money to a specific person or organization. I mentioned in Chapter 8 how bailing someone out financially over and over without helping them stop their chronic dependence is being unloving. I might add that this kind of support could very well be cruel, enabling them to stay in a dire situation.

Another word for kindness is compassion which is defined: "a strong feeling of sympathy for people who are suffering and a desire to help them."[2] Being kind is not about you; it's about the well-being of others. Cruelty is the opposite of compassion. It is defined: "behavior that causes pain or suffering to others, especially deliberately."[3] Therefore, you are inhumane when you don't practice kindness.

Kindness would have you teach them, possibly spending your time instead of money, pointing them towards freedom. Or it could mean giving monetarily but not directly, paying their rehab center fees or for a counselor. Always listen to the prompting from the Holy Spirit; true kindness is steeped in patience and prayer.

The most

extraordinary kindness

is when the recipient

doesn't deserve it.

Though it is not about you, there is a principle that I alluded to at the start: Do unto others as you would have them do unto you. This tenet is commonly called the Golden Rule, and it is derived from Luke 6:31 and Matthew 7:12. The fruit of the Spirit certainly has a reciprocal effect. **"The merciful man doeth good to his own soul**: but he that is cruel troubleth his own flesh" (Proverbs 11:17). So, don't take kindness lightly.

Being merciful is the most beautiful and ultimate way of being kind. As opposed to grace, which is giving what someone doesn't deserve, mercy is withholding what someone deserves. At a time in which people seem to be quick to blame and condemn, mercy seems to be an alien concept.

When someone seems to have nothing but money trouble, I ask questions to learn more about their financial hand and feet, specifically kindness. As Proverb 11:17 implies, the lack of kindness can bring difficulty. The antidote is to be merciful and receive goodness in return. Never do the right thing for selfish reasons, but know that God's promises never return void.

Goodness

The Greek work for Goodness is agathosune, which is translated "uprightness of heart and life."[4] You certainly need good feet to stand upright, and once again, this fruit of the Spirit is related to the heart. Read Psalm 112 for an example of the life of one who is upright, showing generosity and compassion in one's ways. Also, you will find there a promise of wealth and riches to the one who is full of goodness because God is always faithful.

Another definition of goodness is moral excellence. Humanity has a morality problem, where so many people are starving around the world, and those with the means look the other way. And the issue starts with people not acknowledging God as Creator and Judge.

If one doesn't believe in God, they don't recognize His laws, which He gave us for our well-being. Therefore, the question arises, "What is good and what is evil?" Without a lawmaker, you can't tell who's a lawbreaker. It's up to each individual to determine what goodness is.

However, you, because you understand your relationship with God, don't have this problem. He will give you the wisdom to use His great wealth for the good of others once you know your role as manager. Unlike one who doesn't believe the Bible, you seek to obey Romans 12:21: "Be not overcome of evil, but **overcome evil with good**."

Their proper perspective of ownership, obedience, and lawfulness is a topic which I will go into much deeper in *God's Ownership Meets Money Management*.

Goodness spans your life in so many ways, not only in the use of wealth God has placed in your hands. Apply it as well to the talent God has given your hands and feet.

You have unique gifts. You can make things that others can't because that is part of your purpose.

You can give a lot without spending a penny. Giving your time, for example, can be a gift worth more than money could ever supply. Sharing your talent could mean teaching someone to fish as opposed to just giving them fish. The fruit of goodness encompasses all that is charitable and, at the same time, goes far beyond monetary giving.

Kelly Wise Valdes writes,

> *The Bible tells us that the word "good" actually means holy, pure and righteousness. Literally goodness is godliness. Goodness can often be seen in our actions, but our heart also has to be pure. The goodness of Christ is to be demonstrated in our lives every day. Psalm 23:6 says, "Surely goodness and mercy shall follow me all the days of my life, and I shall dwell in the house of the Lord forever."*
>
> *God calls us to be filled with goodness from the inside out, being holy in what we do and say because Christians should have a heart that seeks goodness. We are not to just do good works, because doing good works without a good heart is empty. The "goodness" described as a fruit of the Spirit is not merely moral behavior, but an excellence of character.*[5]

Once again, you can see that all the fruit of the Spirit are tied together and are interdependent, just like our bodies. God is an orderly Creator, so we realize many parallels.

In the following scripture, just like our physical work, we must press through difficult times, for the reward is great.

Paul writes, "And **let us not be weary in well doing**: for in due season we shall reap if we faint not. As we have therefore opportunity, **let us do good unto all men**, especially unto them who are of the household of faith" (Galatians 6:9-10).

Yes, of course, we live in a sowing and reaping world. Sow goodness, and you will reap goodness. Adam and Eve and their two sons, Cain and Abel, learned this lesson of sowing and reaping at the beginning of history.

Galatians 6:7 states: "Be not deceived; God is not mocked: for **whatsoever a man soweth, that shall he also reap.**" Of course, don't do good only to receive a reward, but know that God sees your good works.

You may see how God can use your financial hands and feet to do so many good things, but that is not even the half of it. Your goodness leads to a much greater purpose. And, if you want to do the work of goodness, kindness, and patience in secret, I would like to encourage you not to shy away from letting your light shine in public.

Jesus says: "Ye are the light of the world. A city that is set on an hill cannot be hid. Neither do men light a candle, and put it under a bushel, but on a candlestick; and it giveth light unto all that are in the house. **Let your light so shine before men, that they may see your good works, and glorify your Father which is in heaven**" (Matthew 5:14-16).

The ultimate reward is to see someone come to Christ and glorify the Father because of your good works. Smiles are great. Thank-yous are much appreciated. But to witness someone bow their knee and join the family of believers is priceless. Your financial hands and feet cannot do any greater good than this.

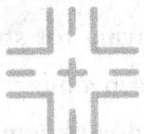

CHAPTER TEN

Your Financial Head

"Keep your head up," is what we often say to encourage someone who's down. But, how do you keep your financial head up when life is happening all around you? Lean on the Master. "But thou, O Lord, art a shield for me; my glory, and the lifter up of mine head" (Psalm 3:3).

This is where financial empowerment, knowledge and wisdom reside. Your head sends the signal to your heart which keeps it beating. It tells your hand and feet where to go and what to do.

The brain is the most complex and powerful supercomputer ever created. God is an amazing Engineer.

From calculations to emotions, your head is where the strategy happens. However, when God is not in control, things may go awry. Let Him be Lord of all, and everything is going to be all right.

The three fruit of the Spirit found here are the ones I previously used to think least about: faithfulness, meekness, and self-control. I knew they existed, but I never found myself praying for strength in this area. No wonder I ended up in such a mess.

Don't worry if you don't know where to start, for as a Christian, the Holy Spirit promises to be with you, teach you, and guide you each step of the way. Faithfulness guides your plan, pointing it in the right direction. Meekness keeps you focused on the target. Self-control helps your judgment so that your actions are right on time.

"For to be carnally minded is death; but to be spiritually minded is life and peace" (Romans 8:6).

When working in the corporate world, there were always times when the managers needed guidance. No matter if there were questions about the strategy, a need to know the next steps, or if there was an issue, everyone knew where to go for answers and direction.

Go to the head of the company. In everyday life and financial strategy, the head is always the Father, and His door is always open. We can get our financial head together by going to the Head of All. And we have direct access through the Son.

As you proceed through the last three fruit of the spirit, ask the Lord to reveal intricate details of His plan and mission for your life.

Faithfulness

You must be a faithful manager. An owner has the right to give you less to manage or, if you are entirely unfaithful, take it all away.

In sports, there is an expression: "Have your head in the game." It alludes to the fact that you can physically be there going through all the motions, but you are not being faithful to your position and doing your part as a team player. The same goes for your financial head.

Don't get this confused with head knowledge or intellect. No super high IQ is necessary. In fact, people who tend to over-think struggle the most. I know because I was one of them. The best financial strategy only requires God's wisdom and about a 3rd grader's knowledge of math. Many people throw their hands up and say that creating a financial plan is just too complicated, or they don't understand how to get started. That is most likely because they have not been shown a method that empowers them.

See, just like everything in life, there is a super sophisticated way, and then there is the straightforward strategy. Pay no attention to books and courses that have fancy jargon and advanced charts and graphs. Using your financial head only requires intentionality, faith, and a simple, straightforward strategy.

What are you doing with the wealth God has allowed you to manage? Have you given this deep thought?

> *Who then is a faithful and wise servant, whom his lord hath made ruler over his household, to give them meat in due season? Blessed is that servant, whom his lord when he cometh shall find so doing. Verily I say unto you, That he shall make him ruler over all his goods. But and if that evil servant shall say in his heart, My lord delayeth his coming; And shall begin to smite his fellowservants, and to eat and drink with the drunken; The lord of that servant shall come in a day when he looketh not for him, and in an hour that he is not aware of, And shall cut him asunder, and appoint him his portion with the hypocrites: there shall be weeping and gnashing of teeth (Matthew 24:45-51).*

Wow! Those words of Jesus are powerful, impactful, and a bit alarming. There are repercussions if He finds you not faithful. You should not fear, for you now know that His words give you the Wisdom you need to manage well.

You will never be perfect, but you must continue to study the Bible daily, surround yourself with like-minded individuals, and pray always for every decision as you grow as a child of God. The first words in the passage describe the manager as faithful and wise. So you must seek God's wisdom alongside managing His wealth.

Three of the areas in which God calls us to be faithful are Spending, Saving, and Giving. In all these tasks, you must be faithful; you must use your head. When you are married, being financially faithful means having regular budget meetings with your spouse, thinking through current situations and future plans. As a single person, it may mean having a monthly meeting scheduled with your accountability partner to share your thoughts about your personal money management. To neglect engaging in intentional deep thought and discussions concerning this area of life would result in being an unfaithful manager.

Use your financial head when spending, planning, and optimizing the outgo from God's resources: "**He that is faithful in that which is least is faithful also in much**: and he that is unjust in the least is unjust also in much. And if ye have not been faithful in that which is another man's, who shall give you that which is your own?" (Luke 16:10, 12)

I have met far too many people who err by saying, "I don't have enough money to budget." Or they may say, "Once I make X amount of money, then I will think about creating a plan." Are they being lazy, unwise, undisciplined? Maybe, I don't know. But I do know they are unfaithful.

The truth is, they have little because they don't manage what little they have. Your habits with a small amount in the bank directly translate to what your actions would be with one hundred times as much.

While teaching my students and coaching my clients, I always begin with the budget from day one because it is the only way to be faithful. This is not a book about how to budget, but I would like to explain to you why you should budget.

God expects for you to channel the currency in your possession in a direction that flows according to His will for your life. To do otherwise would to be unfaithful. Through prayer and your determination, all financial matters work out according to the plan. This goes for every human being, rich or poor.

Start with prayer and end with a plan by strategically saving and investing for the future: Read the story of the talents in Matthew 25. Here is an excerpt: "He that had received five talents sayeth, Lord, thou deliveredst unto me five talents: behold, I have gained beside them five talents more. His lord said unto him, **Well done, thou good and faithful servant: thou hast been faithful over a few things**, I will make thee ruler over many things: enter thou into the joy of thy lord" (Matthew 25:20-21).

In the King James version of the Bible, Galatians lists this fruit of the Spirit as "faith." You must have faith to be faithful. If you have no faith in God, you become a Scrooge, holding on tightly to every penny. Faithfulness is living in financial freedom, which brings about peace and joy that helps your heart. Remember how interconnected your head and heart are.

This is the reason the word "FAITH" is the largest word on the cover of this book. It is the only mindset that truly leads one to the ultimate financial strategy. Faith, and not any faith, but Biblical Faith is found at the precise point where God's Wealth and God's Wisdom intersect.

Gentleness (Meekness)

Have you ever known someone for quite some time and later learned that they are incredibly wealthy? They were not secretive about it; they just didn't flaunt it. They were meek, in other words, humble.

God will provide you with all that you need and then some, but not if He knows you cannot handle it. That would be cruel. There is no loving parent who would give a one-year-old a hacksaw. And I thank Master God, He didn't allow me to have a million-dollar net worth to manage fifteen years ago when I was still trying to do things my way. I would have blown most of it for sure.

The world system is the opposite. You may notice some ungodly people who get wealthy, and then slowly get destroyed by the way they live their lives. Of course, this doesn't happen with everyone. Some never get rich in any way, but in their very act of chasing riches they erode God's true purpose for their life.

Being meek

means knowing that

net worth

does not equate with

self-worth.

The question I had to ask myself is, does it really matter what others are doing when I should only be concerned with what God has for my life? Of course, the answer is no.

Humbleness requires that you know that you are not the owner; you are just the one who stewards the assets. Being meek means knowing that net worth does not equate with self-worth. Gentleness creates a character in you that treats everyone the same, no matter how much money they make (or don't make).

Some people who don't have much try to look rich because they think it matters. Other have great riches and try to look poor because they are embarrassed by their success. However, those with a proper mindset apply God's wisdom to the massive wealth He has given them. Didn't Jesus say: "**Blessed are the meek**: for they shall inherit the earth" (Matthew 5:5).

"Meekness is not weakness," writes Pastor Greg Laurie. "It is power under constraint."[1] Having money can be powerful and can affect your financial head by being either beneficial or detrimental. Don't let your financial head get big. The world may see meekness as weakness, but we Christians understand the power behind that word.

When asked if they want riches together with honor and long life, most people would say "Absolutely!" But they walk away once they realize how difficult it is to obtain those things with righteousness. They are dismayed because they want fame and glory. But the Bible says, "**By**

humility and the fear of the Lord are riches, and honour, and life" (Proverbs 22:4).

Take note that the word "humility" is not humiliation; it is the same as meekness. And the phrase "fear of the Lord" is not fear, as in the boogie man sense; no, it means reverence and respect for God's authority.

The gentlest man ever to walk the earth was Jesus. Look to His example as the way to be the most gentle, meek, and humble person. The Bible urges us likewise: **"Let nothing be done through strife or vainglory;** but in lowliness of mind let each esteem other better than themselves. Look not every man on his own things, but every man also on the things of others. Let this mind be in you, which was also in Christ Jesus" (Philippians 2:3-5).

In the Old Testament, Numbers 12:3 describes Moses as "very meek, above all the men which were upon the face of the earth." That is a high honor. Why did the Bible describe Moses in this manner?

Looking at Moses' upbringing, we see that he was raised in the lap of luxury in Pharaoh's palace. He had the best of food, clothing, education, and training. Moses must not have wanted for much throughout his younger years.

But he didn't let it get to his head. Moses kept his ear tuned to the will of God in his life. When God spoke to him, he listened, he obeyed, he forsook all the luxury with which he was accustomed, and he humbly led his people away from slavery.

Llewellyn Martin writes:

> *Moses had the prime opportunity in a rich culture to make his fortune without a lot of work. According to secular history, he was already constructing buildings for himself. He was headed toward being a Pharaoh where everyone works to build your kingdom. Instead, he gave that all up to slave away for God's people without any financial benefits. The only way he could accomplish this was to see beyond this life to the eternal rewards awaiting him. We need to learn to see beyond this world's temporal riches to eternal wealth.[2]*

Would you be so meek as not to pursue a sure path towards huge personal financial gain, but instead preferring to follow God's plan for your life even though you were uncertain of the outcome?

Also, don't believe that you must be poor to exercise this fruit of the spirit. There are many gentle, humble and meek women and men who are following the will of God while generating great riches. The real question you and I have to ask ourselves is, are we willing to give up anything to follow the Master's plan?

This fruit of the spirit will change everything you do and the reason you do it. There is nothing like asking God for His direction in every single aspect of your life. You will be on an adventure of a lifetime, and your financial head will be blown away. God, in his infinite wisdom, has plans you know not of, and you can only live out that plan if you gently and meekly follow the Great Shepherd.

Self-Control (Temperance)

When I mentioned that I personally battle with two of the nine fruit, do you guess which one was the second? Yes, this is it. Don't judge me.

Paul mentions how we all struggle in this area: "For I know that in me (that is, in my flesh,) dwelleth no good thing: for to will is present with me; but **how to perform that which is good I find not**" (Romans 7:18).

I've already admitted to impulse buying a timeshare. But my lack of self-control has gone far beyond that incident. The decisions that I made in the early 2000s were all rash, all without prayer, and without patience. As a result, I found myself in almost $150,000 of debt, not including the house.

On top of that, I found myself gambling. No, not the casino or lottery-type, but putting money into risky investments. The professionals call it speculation. Long story short, I lost my pants.

If you have done any of these things with money, I just want you to know that you are not alone. And I also wanted to let you know that there is hope because, thank God, the Lord is patient with us even when we don't exercise self-control.

This is the quintessential financial head problem. We think we are smarter than Biblical truths; but we are not. It is still best to use God's wisdom with His wealth. If you want to concentrate your prayers on one of these nine fruit first, choose this one, because once you have strong temperance in your life, the other fruit of the Spirit grow faster. Of course, the opposite is also true. "A person without self-control is like a city with broken-down walls" (Proverbs 25:28 NLT).

I learned my lesson about impulsive buying. We should all avoid forming the bad habit of impulse shopping, which is spending on activities or items outside our plan. Window shopping is not a good idea when you have no guardrails in your head (or your heart, for that matter).

And this goes beyond shopping malls. I've seen people get house fever, buying a home far outside their budget and their needs. Doing this could not only make you "house poor," and be in a situation where you can't buy basic needs because of the mortgage; this could affect your marriage and your job.

Another area you need to use your head is to avoid swindlers, bad investments, and business schemes. The Holy Spirit has a way of giving you a sense of caution when you walk into the place of a con artist. You know instinctively when a salesperson is trying to get one over on you. These invitations come by telephone, text message, and email too. So be vigilant.

"Enter not into the path of the wicked, and **go not in the way of evil men**. Avoid it, pass not by it, turn from it, and pass away. For they sleep not, except they have done mischief; and their sleep is taken away, unless they cause some to fall" (Proverbs 4:14-16).

Above all, do not spend money on immoral things. This crucial area of self-control has been the downfall of many. Gambling, drugs, and sex top the list of improper ways to spend God's wealth. Read Proverbs 7, where Solomon warns his sons about prostitutes.

The Bible warns us about the days we live in right now and how the lack of self-control will damage our relationship with God. "This know also, that in the last days perilous times shall come. For men shall be **lovers of their own selves, covetous, boasters, proud**, blasphemers, disobedient to parents, **unthankful**, unholy, Without natural affection, trucebreakers, false accusers, **incontinent**, fierce, **despisers of those that are good**, Traitors, heady, highminded, **lovers of pleasures** more than lovers of God" (2 Timothy 3:1-4).

Though self-control is the last of the nine fruit of the Spirit, it is no less important than the rest. Notice in that passage how there is covetousness (lovers of money), pride, despisers of goodness, and, of course, spending money on pleasure instead of righteous living.

Interestingly, modern translations mention "without self-control" instead of the word "incontinent." I like the picture that the old King James English presents. When I was living with no financial self-control, my life looked (and smelled) like a pile of poop.

Please, promise me you will not be a part of those on this list.

I want to wrap up this part of the book by mentioning the ultimate way to have self-control. You must use this essential tool to demonstrate all nine fruit of the Spirit. Of course, I'm talking about your budget.

The budget creates a healthy atmosphere for wealth to be orchestrated as God leads you in earning, spending, saving, investing, giving, and receiving. If you don't budget every month before the month begins, you need to form this habit today. "For **which of you, intending to build a tower, sitteth not down first, and counteth the cost,** whether he have sufficient to finish it? Lest haply, after he hath laid the foundation, and is not able to finish it, all that behold it begin to mock him, Saying, This man began to build, and was not able to finish" (Luke 14:28-30).

Finish strong. You need to have a Godly plan.

Don't forget to grab a copy of the **Biblical Faith Meets Financial Strategy—Finances by the Fruit of the Spirit** poster on the INTERSECTION Resource Page: intersection.zeroinfinancial.com[3]

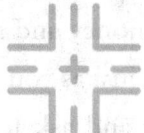

Freedom at the Intersection

God is so good and teaches us so much about handling all the resources He has made available for us to use. Now, you can grow and give this wealth for His Glory.

Returning full circle to the most important decision one can make in life, I want to make sure you have surrendered all to Jesus Christ, the King of everything. Many books, especially those on finances, tuck this information in the last chapter or appendix of its pages. But I wanted to make sure it was the first subject because that is where it rightfully belongs.

Though I implore you to make this essential decision presented in Chapter 1, you may have skipped through those paragraphs to read the rest of the book. I pray you now see the significance of this choice for your entire life, finances included. And if you have not made Jesus your Lord and Savior, I ask that you consider this choice right now.

Salvation costs no money and results in true freedom. God wants you to come just as you are, baggage and all. All you have to do is pray and ask Jesus to come into your heart, and He will. Your life will never be the same.

Like I said in Chapter 1, if you have made this decision today, I would like to know, plus I would like to send you a resource to help you with your walk with Christ. Go to salvation.zeroinfinancial.com to declare your decision to follow Jesus.[1]

Congratulations! All of Heaven is rejoicing and celebrating this moment. Jesus said, **"There is joy in the presence of the angels of God over one sinner that repenteth"** (Luke 15:10b). Welcome to the family!

Your next step is to apply all the principles in this book to your financial strategy. You now have freedom as a child of God. Your relationship with God the Father, Son, and Holy Spirit will lead you to greater purpose, greater satisfaction, and greater joy.

Now that you understand that church is full of imperfect people like you and me, helping each other as we aim to live and grow at the intersection, you can appreciate meeting and worshiping together. As you read the Bible, knowing that God will speak to you specifically about all your financial concerns and desires, you will fall in love with the Word. Prayer will become a powerful weapon against worry and anxiety.

The Holy Spirit's guidance will help you grow in wealth and wisdom. And the Fruit of the Spirit will inject love, joy, peace, patience, kindness, goodness, faithfulness, gentleness, and self-control into every dollar you spend, give, and save.

I hope you have enjoyed this book and these fundamental principles of financial living according to the Bible. That is what it looks like when you are living according to the riches of the Word of God.

Read *God's Ownership Meets Money Management* next where you'll see how God the Owner intersects with you, the manager. It contains some extremely important truths, examples, and guidance from the Holy Scripture, all of which come with promises of blessing as well as warnings of judgment. It always works out best when we do it God's way.

Now, go zero in on your financial target at the INTERSECTION where God's Wealth meets God's Wisdom.

Free Resources

To help you Zero In on the INTERSECTION where God's Wealth meets God's Wisdom, download the free resources from the INTERSECTION Resource Page:

intersection.zeroinfinancial.com

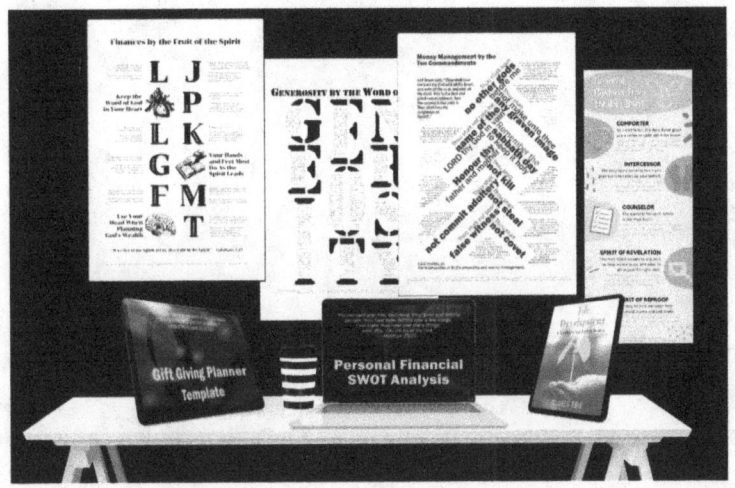

- **BOOK:** Life Development—A New Believer's Guide to Growing in Christ

- **INFOGRAPHIC:** Financial Guidance from the Holy Spirit

- **POSTER:** Finances by the Fruit of the Spirit

- **WORKBOOK:** Personal Financial SWOT Analysis

- **POSTER:** Money Management by the Ten Commandments

- **WORKBOOK:** Gift Giving Planner Template

- **POSTER:** Generosity by the Word of God

Thank You!

To all those who have been so generous to financially support the creation of this book series, I am so thankful. You helped bring INTERSECTION to fruition.

Forward Church Myrtle Beach

Kuba Wyrobek

Clovers & Val McWilliams

Carlos & Maria Correa

Ellie Markova

Anton & Aleksandra Zhloba

Pastor Chris, Heather, & Nelson Honeycutt

Dr. Anthony Jenkins

Pastor Allen & Debbie Causey

D.S. & Stella Wilson

D. Greg & Susie Ebie

David & Kelly Franco

Nicholas Ryan Rendleman

Kaffa Morales

Scott Petrarca

Marcos & Mireya Bernal

Angel Christopher

Pastor Steve & Jessica Mueller

Nick Kolovos

Anibal & Joelia Maldonado

David Gumins

J. Varghese

Linda Ostrowski

Steve & Traci Hickman

Richard L. Dobbins, Jr.

Pastor Edgar & Christie Rivas

Christian Baird

John Kuntharayil

Vuong Dinh

Chaplain James F. Burling

Adele van der Lecq

Edgar Rios

Note from the Author: Reviews are gold to authors! If you have enjoyed this book, would you consider reviewing it on your favorite book retailer's website? Thank you!

Notes

Introduction: Taking Aim

1 Pickus, Abigail. "A Coach In Your Corner." Chicago Tribune, December 17, 2000. https://www.chicagotribune.com/news/ctxpm-2000-12-17-0012170504-story.html

Chapter One: Live in Christ Jesus

1 Ritenbaugh, John W. "Passover, Obligation, and Love." Bible Tools, March 1994. https://www.bibletools.org/index.cfm/fuseaction/Library.sr/CT/PERSONAL/k/602/Passover-Obligation-Love.htm

2 Bowling, Ted E. "Sticks and Stones." Bible Tools, December 2003. https://www.bibletools.org/index.cfm/fuseaction/Library.sr/CT/RA/k/861/Sticks-Stones.htm

3 Poonen, Zac. "Let Christ Be the Centre of Your Life." Christian Fellowship Church, Bangalore, June 21, 2020. https://cfcindia.com/wftw/let-christ-be-the-centre-of-your-life

4 "Sinner's Prayer." In *Wikipedia*, December 27, 2021. https://en.wikipedia.org/wiki/Sinner%27s_prayer#Billy_Graham

5 McWilliams, Johnny. "Dedicating Your Life to Jesus." Zero In Financial. Accessed January 15, 2022. https://zeroinfinancial.com/salvation/

6 Oxford Advanced American Dictionary. "Ransom | Definition." Accessed January 15, 2022. https://www.oxfordlearnersdictionaries.com/definition/american_english/ransom_1

Chapter Two: Not So Religious

1 Lawrence, Brother. *The Practice of the Presence of God.* Springdale, PA.: Whitaker House, 1982.

2 Chery, Fritz. "Religion Vs Relationship With God: 4 Biblical Truths To Know." Bible Reasons, November 15, 2021. https://biblereasons.com/religion-vs-relationship-with-god

3 Geisler, Norman L., and Frank Turek. *I Don't Have Enough Faith to Be an Atheist.* Wheaton, Illinois: Crossway Books, 2004.

4 CompellingTruth.org. "What Proof Do We Have for the Inspiration of the Bible?" Accessed July 20, 2020. https://www.compellingtruth.org/proof-inspiration-Bible.html

5 Blue, Ron, and Michael Blue. *God Owns It All: Finding Contentment and Confidence In Your Finances.* Lifeway Press, 2016.

6 McWilliams, Johnny. "Zero In Financial Press | INTERSECTION." Zero In Financial. Accessed April 4, 2020. https://zeroinfinancial.com/press/intersection/

7 Alcorn, Randy. *Heaven: A Comprehensive Guide to Everything the Bible Says About Our Eternal Home.* Carol Stream, Illinois: Tyndale Momentum, 2007

Chapter Three: You Need People

1 National Institute on Aging. "Social Isolation, Loneliness in Older People Pose Health Risks," April 23, 2019. http://www.nia.nih.gov/news/social-isolation-loneliness-older-people-pose-health-risks

Chapter Four: Pray First

1 Jordan, William. *A Tithe of Time.* Laguna Hills, California: Pursuit Publishing, 2013

2 Knowing Jesus. "What Does Isaiah 40:31 Mean?" Accessed January 6, 2020. https://dailyverse.knowing-jesus.com/isaiah-40-31

3 McWilliams, Johnny. "Zero In On This." Zero In Financial. Accessed January 15, 2022. https://zeroinfinancial.com/blog/

Chapter Five: Don't Worry

[1] Swindoll, Chuck. "The Subtle Enemy of Simple Faith." Insight for Living Ministries, 1988. https://insight.org/resources/insights-to-individual/SPF-worry

[2] Mears, Dr. Henrietta C. *What The Bible Is All About: New International Version, Bible Handbook.* Carol Stream, Illinois: Tyndale House Publishers, 2016

[3] Ebie, D. Greg. *Resurrected Faith: The Heart of a Contender.* Firm Foundation Publishing, 2021

[4] Tepper, Taylor. "Most Americans Don't Have Enough Savings To Cover A $1K Emergency | Bankrate.Com." Bankrate, January 18, 2018. https://www.bankrate.com/banking/savings/financialsecurity-0118/

[5] Adams, Laura. "How Much Can You Save on Auto Insurance by Raising Your Deductible?" HuffPost, January 10, 2017. https://www.huffpost.com/entry/how-much-can-you-save-on-_b_14084854

[6] Alcorn, Randy. *Heaven: A Comprehensive Guide to Everything the Bible Says About Our Eternal Home.* Carol Stream, Illinois: Tyndale Momentum, 2007

Chapter Six: Be Happy

[1] Edwards, Jonathan, and Mark R. Valeri. *Sermons and Discourses, 1730-1733.* The Works of Jonathan Edwards, v. 17. New Haven: Yale University Press, 1999

[2] Oxford Advanced Learner's Dictionary. "Opportunity Cost | Definition." Accessed March 13, 2020. https://www.oxfordlearnersdictionaries.com/us/definition/english/opportunity-cost?q=opportunity+cost

[3] Bradley, Dr. Anne. "What 'No Free Lunch' Means for Biblical Stewardship." Institute for Faith, Work & Economics, February 17, 2017. https://tifwe.org/what-no-free-lunch-means-for-biblicalstewardship

Chapter Seven: Your Financial Vital Signs

[1] Johns Hopkins Medicine. "Vital Signs (Body Temperature, Pulse Rate, Respiration Rate, Blood Pressure)." Accessed July 4, 2020. https://www.hopkinsmedicine.org/health/conditions-and-diseases/vital-signs-body-temperature-pulse-rate-respiration-rate-bloodpressure

[2] Petruzzello, Melissa. "Mammon | Definition." Encyclopedia Britannica, September 8, 2020. https://www.britannica.com/topic/mammon

[3] Infinium Medical. "4 Very Important Reasons Why Vital Signs Monitoring Matters," December 9, 2020. https://www.infiniummedical.com/vital-signs-monitoring/

[4] McWilliams, Johnny. "Zero In Financial Press | INTERSECTION." Zero In Financial. Accessed April 4, 2020. https://zeroinfinancial.com/press/intersection

Chapter Eight: Your Financial Heart

[1] Brouhard, Rod. "How Long Does Brain Activity Last After Cardiac Arrest?" Verywell Health, September 30, 2021. https://www.verywellhealth.com/brain-activity-after-cardiacarrest-1298429

[2] US Navy SURFPAC. "USS Milius DDG-69." Accessed May 24, 2020. https://www.surfpac.navy.mil/Ships/USS-Milius-DDG-69/About-Us/

[3] Szoldra, Paul. "19 of the Coolest Military Unit Mottos." *We Are The Mighty* (blog), December 24, 2021. https://www.wearethemighty.com/popular/military-mottos/

[4] McWilliams, Johnny. "Zero In On This | Generously Give." Zero In Financial. Accessed April 4, 2020. https://zeroinfinancial.com/generouslygive

[5] McCraty, Rollin. *Science of the Heart: Exploring the Role of the Heart in Human Performance.* Vol. 2. Boulder Creek, Calif.: HeartMath Research Center, Institute of HeartMath, 2015

Chapter Nine: Your Financial Hands and Feet

[1] Barhum, Lana. "What Are the Symptoms of Poor Circulation?" Medical News Today, January 17, 2020. https://www.medicalnewstoday.com/articles/322371

[2] Oxford Advanced American Dictionary. "Compassion | Definition." Accessed April 11, 2020. https://www.oxfordlearnersdictionaries.com/us/definition/american_english/compassion

[3] Oxford Advanced American Dictionary. "Cruelty | Definition." Accessed April 11, 2020. https://www.oxfordlearnersdictionaries.com/us/definition/american_english/cruelty

[4] Bible Tools. "Agathosune - Greek/Hebrew Definitions." Accessed June 5, 2020. https://www.bibletools.org/index.cfm/fuseaction/Lexicon.show/ID/G19/agathosune.htm

[5] Valdes, Kelly Wise. "The Fruit Of The Holy Spirit: What Is Goodness?" *Osprey Observer* (blog), September 2, 2020. https://www.ospreyobserver.com/2020/09/the-fruit-of-the-holy-spiritwhat-is-goodness/

Chapter Ten: Your Financial Head

[1] Laurie, Greg. "Greg Laurie Daily Devotion." Crosswalk, September 22, 2010. https://www.crosswalk.com/devotionals/harvestdaily/greg-laurie-daily-devotionsept-22-2010-11638452.html

[2] Martin, Llewellyn. "Moses The Meekest Man." Pilgrim Ministry, June 2011. https://www.pilgrimministry.org/literature/moses-themeekest-man

[3] McWilliams, Johnny. "Zero In Financial Press | INTERSECTION." Zero In Financial. Accessed April 4, 2020. https://zeroinfinancial.com/press/intersection

Conclusion: Freedom at the Intersection

[1] McWilliams, Johnny. "Dedicating Your Life to Jesus." Zero In Financial. Accessed January 15, 2022. https://zeroinfinancial.com/salvation/

About the Author

Johnny McWilliams, founder of Zero In Financial LLC, guides his students, customers, and clients as they RECOVER from past money mistakes, GROW your present pocketbook position, and ZERO IN on your future financial fortune, ultimately leaving a lasting legacy of love. After working as a tax preparer, dissecting the details of credit scoring and reporting, passing various exams and licensure, including Series 7, Series 66, life & health insurance, and real estate broker, Johnny realized the average American's need for financial coaching, education, and inspiration.

Once Johnny completed ten years of enlistment in the United States Navy, graduated with a Master of Business Administration, worked as a property & casualty insurance consultant, and became certified as a Ramsey Solutions Master Financial Coach, he began guiding individuals and families to Zero In on their financial target.

Johnny and his wife, Christine, have been married for over twelve years, and they are blessed with one married son, one married daughter, and no grandchildren yet.